# A Guide to Visual Anthropology

# A Guide to Visual Anthropology

**Jayasinhji Jhala**
Temple University

Contributors:

Elizabeth Noznesky
Cary Million
Lindsey Powell

 **Wadsworth Publishing Company**
I(T)P® An International Thomson Publishing Company

Belmont, CA • Albany, NY • Bonn • Boston • Cincinnati
Detroit • Johannesburg • London • Madrid • Melbourne • Mexico City
New York • Paris • Singapore • Tokyo • Toronto • Washington

COPYRIGHT © 1998 by Wadsworth Publishing Company
A Division of International Thomson Publishing Inc.
I(T)P® The ITP logo is a registered trademark under license.

Printed in the United States of America
1 2 3 4 5 6 7 8 9 10

For more information, contact Wadsworth Publishing Company,
10 Davis Drive, Belmont, CA 94002, or electronically at
http://www.thomson.com/wadsworth.html

| | |
|---|---|
| International Thomson<br>Publishing Europe<br>Berkshire House 168-173<br>High Holborn<br>London, WC1V 7AA, England | International Thomson<br>Publishing GmbH<br>Königswinterer Strasse 418<br>53227 Bonn, Germany |
| Thomas Nelson Australia<br>102 Dodds Street<br>South Melbourne 3205<br>Victoria, Australia | International Thomson<br>Publishing Asia<br>221 Henderson Rd.<br>#05-10 Henderson Building<br>Singapore 0315 |
| Nelson Canada<br>1120 Birchmount Road<br>Scarborough, Ontario<br>Canada M1K 5G4 | International Thomson<br>Publishing Japan<br>Hirakawacho Kyowa bldg, 3F<br>2-2-1 Hirakawacho<br>Chiyoda-ku, Tokyo 102, Japan |
| International Thomson<br>Publishing Southern Africa<br>Building 18, Constantia Park<br>240 Old Pretoria Road<br>Halfway House, 1685 South Africa | International Thomson<br>Editores<br>Campos Eliseos 385, Piso 7<br>Col Polanco<br>11560 México D.F. México |

ISBN 0-534-53932-7

# INTRODUCTION

This *Guide to Visual Anthropology* presents commentary on fifty-one films for the Teaching of Introductory Social Anthropology.

There is a growing recognition that a considerable portion of our knowledge about the cultures of different societies of the world comes to us through film, video, television, the Internet, and other audio visual media, and that this circumstance is not restricted to persons living in technically sophisticated environments but to individuals and communities in many parts of the world which have a simpler technological circumstance. This powerful educational source augments the traditional oral and written streams of knowledge, and it is in recognizing the tripartite nature of the contemporary information package that this writing seeks to present comments about fifty-one films relevant to the study of social anthropology.

The films have been selected to serve several ideas. Firstly, they are offered to those who would wish to use them to teach introductory cultural anthropology and to use the films to supplement the readings that they consider part of the educational package. As an alternate use, these films could serve as the core texts that are supported by written materials. Thirdly, these films are suggested as a study of cultural content and authorial intent in recognition that both reflexivity and activist agency concerns more and more anthropologists in their doing ethnography and making anthropology. Finally, the study of these films is valuable for the acquisition of critical thinking tools by which to "read" visual texts, not merely for "content" but for "authorial intent." These skills, which once acquired in the anthropology classroom, will hopefully enable the student with a more critical faculty with which to "read" "recreational" and "informative" visual texts offered in the home or workplace, soliciting product and ideology.

This writing builds on the contribution of prior writings and should be seen as adding to that corpus. The comments about each film come from several individuals who have taught introductory anthropology with them at Temple University and are part of the Program for the Anthropology of Visual Communication. Their comments and evaluations are based on their experience in the classroom as well as their experience of these works at other academic forum. The distributors/authors notice regarding these works is included to alert the users about their emphasis on the content of the films and contains information about their reception in the more public arena of film festival exposure and television broadcasting. The alphabetical format for the listing of these visual texts serves to underline the fact that this is not a discreet package to be used in a special way but rather that these films can be used to construct a course or courses that best suit the expertise of individual teachers. It seeks to include those persons who have had no experience with using film in the anthropology classroom as well as those who are anthropologists and makers of visual texts. The comments are suggestive rather than prescriptive and exclusive.

The films selected demonstrate a wide range in their chosen styles and conventions and sketch in part the history of this mode of representation. Some films primarily describe and by description supplement written ethnographic practice. Others make arguments, summaries, and conjectures to promote anthropological discussion. Thus they bring the alien culture through picture and sound to the classroom as well as stimulate discourse from the stimulus within the alien context.

The many approaches adopted in this disciple include what is called observational cinema, cinema verite, participatory cinema, argumentative, provocative, reflexive cinema, and the many hybrid combinations of these textual strategies. The length of these films range from some that are a few minutes long to others that are over one hundred minutes in length and others still that are parts of a more extensive collection of films. The films include biographies, analysis of single events, examination of life styles, migrations, examination of institutions, and conversational engagements.

The subject matter includes gathering and hunting societies, gardening and agricultural societies, pastoral peoples, rural and ruburn and urban societies, and distinct enclaves within urban societies. They include a whole range of anthropological interests that include the study of art, built environment, colonial contact, dance, kinship, law, life patterns, material culture, modern diasporas, music, oral traditions, performance, religious life and ritual, social relations, technology, theater, and war.

The authorship includes anthropologists as filmmakers, anthropologists as collaborators with filmmakers from the western world or from persons trained in the west who are part of the dominant elite in other societies and anthropologists as collaborators with indigenous filmmakers. Other works are by filmmakers who have no training in anthropology, filmmakers who have an anthropological sensibility acquired outside the academy, indigenous filmmakers making locally relevant texts for local and outside audiences. Still other works are made by spokespersons for special interests be they for minority groups inhabiting urban spaces or specific constituencies of local regional, national, or international significance.

Whereas each film and its commentary articulate its particular potential to the teacher and can be interpreted in several ways, it may help some to examine the following suggestions in studying visual texts. What are visual texts? How are they made; what techniques are used, and what strategy is employed and by whom and for what purposes? What is its structure, and what are its components and elements? How is a visual text different from a written text, and what advantages and disadvantages does its nature and use pose for the teacher and student?

One approach has been to analyze films which are complex and composite texts by identifying several discreet strands of information. Many ethnographic films comprise of the classic four strands or streams of information. These are the pictorial stream, the commentary stream, the sound/music stream, and the textual stream of subtitle and intertitle. By examining how each stream provides particular types of information and by assessing how various streams of information are used to compliment each other, it becomes clear how video and filmmakers execute their textual strategy. Knowing what they do and use also provides the teacher some evidence about what authors chose to hide, avoid, or ignore, and this information in turn permits students to better critique these films and learn about the agendas and propensities of the otherwise frequently invisible authors.

Many of the ethnographic films presented here are now thirty or more years old and despite the fact that they were made and presented as contemporary reports from the field they are now historical documents. This requires the user of these films to contextualize them in time as well as in space, so that societies they depict are not seen to be in limbo and in a static cyclical condition.

Nature of viewing or consuming visual texts — private viewing in the privacy of one's room or library booth which is akin to reading a book with its requirement of solitary perusal. Congregational viewing in the classroom, theater, living room, den, or bar makes for a different and more mediated learning experience. Unlike books, visual texts are generally a one time exposure that the student has from which to gain insight and extract information. Even where there is a multiple viewing possibility, films do not have page numbers or time markers that restrict the students ability to refer back and reference material as is common academic practice. The same is true for bibliographical, indexical, and biographical data. With advances in computer technology, this may in time not be a problem but not at the present time — the linear reading of visual texts is a major constraint the teacher must grapple with.

Biographical sketch of text makers is provided to position them in time and to provide the user with some data about motive and method that these persons had and their situationality in the intellectual, social, and political circumstance of their time.

CONTRIBUTORS:     Jayasinhji Jhala, Carey Million, Elizabeth
                   Noznesky, and Lindsey Powell

# A MAN CALLED BEE: STUDYING THE YANOMAMO

Tim Asch, filmmaker; Napoleon Chagnon, anthropologist
Distributor: Documentary Educational Resources
Format: 16mm, 1/2 VHS, 3/4 U-matic, color, 42 minutes
Genre: classic, 1975
Key Words:    Fieldwork, Ethnography, Kinship, Reflexivity,
               Reciprocity, Illustrative Film making, Paradigm

SUMMARY:

*A Man Called Bee* shows how cultural anthropologists do their work.
Anthropologist Napoleon Chagnon collects field data and explores some
of the personal problems he faced in his work with the Yanomamo Indians
of southern Venezuela and northern Brazil. Designed as a companion to
Chagnon's book. (Ref: Chagnon, N.A. Studying the Yanomamo, N.Y.:
Holt, Rinehart & Winston, 1974). From the Yanomamo Series.

REASONS FOR ITS USEFULNESS:

This film can be used in several different ways. As a film which
documents a cultural anthropologist at work, on site, struggling to
overcome various problems relating to the location, the informants, and
various cultural and linguistic differences between teacher and subjects, it
serves as a starting point to discussions of anthropological fieldwork.
Methods of investigation, such as Chagnon's efforts to develop elaborate
kinship charts, are shown to reveal an extensive amount of information
about Yanomamo culture. This sort of reflexive posture, where scientists
reveal the fundamental underlying assumptions of their work, allows the
viewer to critique work more easily. For instance, Chagnon calls the
Yanomamo "the fierce people" and several of the films in this series, some
of which are excerpted herein, depict fighting, when in fact a close reading
of the films suggest other possibilities. Thus it also makes a good film
through which to initiate critical evaluation of the cultural interpretation
that is ethnography. Initiates can begin to see how not only ethnocentric
biases, but also a particular paradigm, can give shape to our

understanding of others. While the fissioning and fusing of villages may well be seen to be driven by the needs of political rivalry, food scarcity and protection, the small clues which indicate the presence of an "outside" world encroaching on the pristine primitive paradise in which this anthropologist works might suggest to viewers other potential sources of pressure. It also serves to remind the viewer who controls the reflexivity and thus to consider what might be missing from the picture.

QUESTIONS BEFORE SCREENING:

1. What is a kinship chart? How are they done? What information can they reveal?
2. What do anthropologists do when they "go to the field?"
3. What is cultural relativity and how do anthropologists attempt to use it?
4. Are indigenous people generally free of pressures from the countries in which they are located?
5. What is meant by the term primitive? What is meant by the term civilized? What kinds of people fit in these categories?

QUESTIONS AFTER SCREENING:

1. Why are kinship charts important to Chagnon's work, and what do they reveal to him?
2. How does Chagnon reciprocate to the Yanomamo in return for what they give him? What do they give him?
3. In what ways are the Yanomamo like/unlike us?
4. What signs did you see in the film that might indicate outside influence and/or pressure upon the Yanomamo?
5. Do these people seem to be more "fierce" or more "primitive" than us?
6. Why do you think the author is so prominently featured in this film?

Distributor: Documentary Educational Resources
*Note*: See distributor information at the end of the book.

* * * * * * * * * *

# A ZENANA

Roger Sandall and Jayasinhji Jhala
Distributor: Documentary Educational Resources
Format: 16mm film, video, color, 36 minutes, 1982
Genre: classic ethnographic film
Key Words: India, Kinship, Gender, Feudalism, Hinduism, Islam

## SUMMARY:

In India, the most secluded section of the palace was the zenana, or women's quarters. Here, until recently, palace women lived behind protective walls and brass doors firmly shut at night. This film is an account of women's life in the zenana of Dhrangadhra, in northern India, the seat of power of the Jhala Rajputs from the eleventh century A.D. until 1947. The film unfolds through songs, dances, and stories of several palace women, including the Maharani (wife of the Maharaja), who is the mother of one of the filmmakers. She and others reflect upon traditional women's roles, the strictness of their former seclusion, and the ideals of women's purity and inner strength.

"Of particular interest is the Maharani"s account of how she left PURDAH (seclusion) in 1967 to help her husband contest state election, and how she too was persuaded to campaign for the election in 1971. One notices how in a photograph of her on that occasion the tail of her SARI passes over the left shoulder in the popular fashion, rather than over the right shoulder in the parochial manner of the zenana..."

Paul Hockings<br>American Anthropologist

## REASONS FOR ITS USEFULNESS:

*A Zenana* is useful in a variety of contexts in learning about anthropology. First, it is a valuable document for teaching about gender and, especially, the changing role of women in the twentieth century. Gender roles are revealed to be historically contingent configurations. In this film, the past and the present are juxtaposed through recollection and storytelling. What was expected of women in Rajput culture in the past is recounted while comparing these responsibilities and motivations from the vantage point of reflection to what is currently the norm.

One also gets a sense of what life is and was like in a Rajput palace. Interviews with court singers and maids are plumbed for what they reveal about interlocking families, service, and living together in a religiously diverse culture.

QUESTIONS BEFORE SCREENING:

1. What are the principles of the Rajput Clan System?
2. How have women's roles changed in various societies in the twentieth century?

QUESTIONS AFTER SCREENING:

1. How does the Maharani think things have changed for women in the zenana?
2. What is the role of the family in contemporary society?

FILMS RELATED BY GEOGRAPHIC OR SUBJECT AREA:

The Bharvad Predicament; Tragada-Bhavai; Whose Paintings?

Distributor: Documentary Educational Resources
*Note*: See distributor information at the end of the book.

* * * * * * * * * * *

# ACROSS THE TRACKS: VLACH GYPSIES IN HUNGARY

Disappearing World Series
Michael Stewart, anthropologist
Distributor: Films Incorporated
Format: video only, rental or sale, color, 52 minutes, 1988
Genre: contemporary
Key Words:    Cultural Anthropology, Roma (Gypsy), Hungary,
                Socialism, Economic Anthropology

SUMMARY:

Set in a village outside the Hungarian town of Gyongyos, this program
follows two Gypsy families struggling to maintain their traditions in a
modern Communist state. Despite the romantic image, life for these
people is harsh and often brutal. They live in near slum conditions and
often are forced to work for poverty-level wages.

REASONS FOR ITS USEFULNESS:

*Across the Tracks: Vlach Gypsies in Hungary* is a particularly valuable
film for anthropologists, because it focuses upon a group of people who,
in this age of political correctness, are still very much maligned and
stereotyped in everyday discourse — even by people who profess
themselves to be nonracists and culturally sensitive. One explanation for
this apparent contradiction is that Roma are rarely understood to be an
ethnic group cohering around the poles of kinship, history, and culture;
instead, Roma are treated as if they were a deviant social group founded
upon a similar chosen lifestyle. Consequently, Roma are often denied the
rights and privileges extended to those groups accorded status as ethnic
minorities. Apart from the fact that many Roma throughout Europe and
North America are discriminated against and often denied basic protection
of their human rights, the violation of their rights poses a serious danger
to all citizens in liberal, democratic states which, in the end, must be

judged by the treatment of their political and socio-economic minorities. As Vaclav Havel once said, the treatment of Roma by the state will be a "litmus test" for the success of democracy [in the Czech Republic].

Although Stewart does not center his film around these issues, per se, his film represents Roma as an ethnic group with a unique and deeply rooted cultural history. Moreover, his film challenges some of the stereotypes of Roma commonly held by North Americans and Western Europeans. For one, it dismisses the notion that Roma are primarily nomadic; indeed, all of the Roma depicted in the film are sedentarized, and many work in nearby factories as wage-laborers. For another, it counteracts the notion that Roma prefer to receive state welfare or run confidence schemes rather than to work at "legitimate" full-time jobs. Instead, the audience learns that not a few of the Roma in the Gyongyos area work as wage laborers in nearby factories, while others do jobs that no one else will perform, such as recycling materials from garbage dumps and selling them as scrap. Indeed, the majority of the film focuses upon the economic activities of its subjects, with particular emphasis on one economic forum wherein the primary actors are Romani rather than Hungarian — namely, horse-trading. Apart from having an advantage over ethnic Hungarians and being a generator of cash income, horse-trading is shown to be an important source of wealth to be tapped during economic crisis, a method of equalizing resources within the Romani community, and, finally, a social entertainment during which Romani men can hone their skills in trade and deal negotiations.

QUESTIONS BEFORE SCREENING:

1.  Who are Roma (Gypsies)?
2.  Name several socio-economic features of a communist mode of production.
3.  In economic terms, what is the difference between wealth and money?
4.  What is a syncretic religion?
5.  What is residential segregation? Why does it happen, and what consequences does it have for the groups who are GEOGRAPHICly separated from each other?

QUESTIONS AFTER SCREENING:

1. Give some examples of interdependence between Roma and ethnic Hungarians.
2. Explain the meaning of "turning money around." What purpose might this serve within the Romani community.
3. Give one example of a state law that prevents Roma from benefiting from some of the economic opportunities made available to ethnic Hungarians.
4. Give 2-3 reasons why many Roma wished/were forced to work outside the official economy during the period of state socialism in Hungary.
5. Briefly explain how Roma in Gyongyos responded to the government's decision to ban the building of new housing in currently inhabited settlements.

FILMS RELATED BY GEOGRAPHIC OR SUBJECT AREA:

!Tan Bakhtale, by Alaina Lemon
Latcho Drom, by Tony Gatlif
Tsiganes Finnois/Finnish Gypsies, by Matti Gronfors, 1985, Finland

Distributor: Films Incorporated
*Note*: See distributor information at the end of the book.

\* \* \* \* \* \* \* \* \* \*

---

## - 4 -

## AMERICAN TONGUES

Louis Alvarez and Andrew Kolker, producer/directors
Distributor: New Day Films
Format: 1/2 VHS, color, 56 minutes, 1988
Genre: contemporary
Key Words:     Dialect, Ways of Speaking, Nonverbal Communication, Speech Group, Identity

## SUMMARY:

Southerners talk too slowly. New Yorkers are rude. New Englanders don't say much at all. Anybody who lives in the U.S. knows the clichés about how people in the various parts of the country handle the English language. Now there's an entertaining, award-winning film that examines the attitudes Americans have about the way they talk. *American Tongues* goes to the streets and the countryside to listen to American English in all its diversity and color. From Boston Brahmins to Black Louisiana teenagers, from Texas cowboys to New York professionals, *American Tongues* elicits funny, perceptive, sometimes shocking, and always telling, comments about our diverse society.

## REASONS FOR ITS USEFULNESS:

This is a humorous film which makes the point that we all have a dialect. By interviewing people from different regions of the U.S., viewers hear and see different ways of speaking a language most of us share. Aside from simply providing authentic language, these regional speakers also provide answers to questions about the way they speak, such as historical factors, group identity, changes over time, and so on. The interviewees also drive the investigation by stereotyping dialects from other regions of the country which are then investigated. Though the film primarily focuses on GEOGRAPHIC differences, those relating to class and race are touched on. The film is lively and light but can serve as a useful starting point for various topics in linguistic anthropology.

## QUESTIONS BEFORE SCREENING:

1. What is the difference between a language and a dialect?
2. Do you speak with a dialect? What features can you name that serve to identify it?
3. What is nonverbal communication? How does it modify what you say?
4. Does the way you say things have an effect on how other people relate to you? How? Do you change the way you say things depending on the circumstance?

5. Can you tell where someone is from by the way they speak? What other sorts of judgments do you make about people based on the way they speak?

QUESTIONS AFTER SCREENING:

1. Do the people in the film all speak the same language? The same dialect?
2. Identify as many different features (lexicon, pronunciation, emphasis, speed, word order, etc.) as you can of speakers with different dialects.
3. What stereotypes do the people in the film have about speakers of different dialects? Are they true? How are the stereotypes identified with the way they speak?
4. What differences in speaking does the film recognize other than regional?
5. Why do you think different groups talk differently than others?

Distributor: New Day Films
*Note:* See distributor information at the end of the book.

* * * * * * * * * *

---

## - 5 -

## AN ARGUMENT ABOUT A MARRIAGE

John Marshall, filmmaker
Distributor: Documentary Educational Resources
Format: 16mm film, video, color, 18 minutes, 1969
Genre: classic ethnographic
Key Words:   Southern Africa, !Kung, Ju/Æhoansi, Hunting and
             Gathering, Kinship

SUMMARY:

In 1955, several Boer farmers used threats and promises to persuade two Ju/Æhoansi bands to work on their farms. After a year, the farmers refused to let the Ju/Æhoansi go. Some managed to escape, including

9

Toma, leader of one band, and /Ti!kay, leader of the other. Women and children of /Ti!kay's band were captured by the farmers and forced to return to the farms at gunpoint. One man, /Qui, returned to the farms to protect his captured wife and other women. While on the farm, /Qui began to live with another woman, Baou, and they had a child together. Baou already had a husband, Tsamgao, but he had escaped with the other men to the Ju/Æhoansi settlement, and seemed unlikely to return to the Boer farm to.find his wife.

Three years later the Marshall expedition was able to persuade the police to free the Ju/Æhoansi people on the farms. Although everyone was pleased to be reunited, trouble soon erupted because both /Qui and Tsamgao claimed Baou as his wife. The argument filmed is complicated in several ways: Baou could not really marry /Qui because she had the same name as /Qui's mother, and such a marriage is considered incestuous. Also, /Qui had previously married another woman and still owed bride-service to her father, an obligation that might last for several more years. Moreover, Baou's original husband, Tsamgao, had been performing bride-service for Baou's father even in her absence, and he felt therefore entitled to live with his wife.

REASONS FOR ITS USEFULNESS:

*An Argument about a Marriage* suggests questions about the impact of European farms on not only the economic but also the social life of the Ju/Æhoansi; about the complexities of marriage rules and bride-service in this kinship system; and about the nature of conflict and its mediation among the Ju/Æhoansi. Despite the interpersonal anger, we see how Toma's skillful intervention prevents this particular conflict from escalating to violence.

QUESTIONS BEFORE SCREENING:

1.  What are the principles of the Ju/Æhoansi kinship system?
2.  What are the social effects of dislocation in Ju/Æhoansi society?
3.  What is the nature of conflict resolution depicted in the film?

QUESTIONS AFTER SCREENING:

1. How do bride-service and kinship reckoning become central issues in the conflict?
2. What is the nature of Toma's relationship to the disputants?

FILMS RELATED BY GEOGRAPHIC OR SUBJECT AREA:

The Hunters; The Meat Fight; A Joking Relationship; Bitter Melons; N/um Tchai; N!ai, The Story of a !Kung Woman; Pull Ourselves Up or Die Out; all by John Marshall.

Reviews: American Anthropologist, Volume 76, Number 3, September 1974, Pg. 681-691, by Patricia Draper.
Associated Reading: The Cinema of John Marshall, edited by Jay Ruby, Philadelphia: Harwood Academic Publishers, 1993;
The Harmless People, Elizabeth Marshall Thomas, New York: Alfred A. Knopf, 1959.

Distributor: Documentary Educational Resources
Note: See distributor information at the end of the book.

* * * * * * * * * * *

## AX FIGHT

Timothy Asch, filmmaker; Napoleon Chagnon, anthropologist
Distributor: Documentary Educational Resources
Format: 16mm, 1/2 inch VHS, 3/4 U-matic, color, 30 minutes, 1975
Genre: classic anthropological
Key Words: Dispute Settlement, Ritual Violence, Kinship

SUMMARY:

This film is about a violent outburst in a Yanomamo village in Southern Venezuela, resulting in a club-and-ax fight. This documentary begins with an unedited record of the event, then moves to a slow-motion replay during which combatants are identified and their behavior explained. Next, an anthropologist explains the kinship structure of the fight and cleavages in local descent groups in the village. Lastly, an edited version of the fight illustrates how strongly intellectual models influence visual perception.

REASONS FOR ITS USEFULNESS:

*Ax Fight* is an important film for many reasons. Though it is not clear that the authors intended it to do so, the film conveys a visual message to anthropological neophytes of the savagery and violence of the "primitive." But by examining details, such as the man who abandons his ax in favor of a less deadly staff to enter the aggression at the same level as everyone else, the uninitiated can begin to see the level of individual control extant as a result of social constraints. Despite the involvement of an entire village in a major dispute, only one person is injured. For those who can be made to understand that their initial reading of the people in this film is based on our own myths, the lesson is an important one.

The revision of an initial impression is reinforced by the film itself, which is constructed in such a way as to reconstruct both how anthropological knowledge is gained and how an ethnographic film is put together. The explanation of the cause of the dispute at the end of the unedited footage is later revised as more information is gathered. The interpretive middle section of the film obviates Chagnon's reorganization of the material following his model of village fissioning along the lines of kinship. In the final cut the organization becomes more subtle, yet by showing the process of its ultimate organization as a finished piece, viewers can gain insight into how the chaos of social interaction becomes interpretive ethnography.

It thus can also be used to illustrate how a particular paradigm shapes our understanding of human interaction, allowing students to develop critical insight. The notion that these people are just naturally violent or fierce can be brought into question. For instance, by taking notice of the presence of several members of the film crew, by noting the origin of the most dangerous weapon present — the axes — and so on, students can begin to think about the wider context in which the Yanomamo exist; the external pressures upon them which might lead to such behaviors as are witnessed in the film.

QUESTIONS BEFORE SCREENING:

1. Dispute resolution in our own society and the nature and levels of violence to which we are accustomed is particularly useful to stimulate later reflection in regard to "civilized" and "uncivilized" violent behaviors. Describe the similarities and differences.
2. What is kinship?

QUESTIONS AFTER SCREENING:

1. What would happen if guns were introduced in the society?
2. Does the use of carpet bombing or napalm or nuclear weapons make violence more "civilized?"
3. How does the presence of nonindigenous people and objects show the Yanomamo's place in a state, regional, and global context?
4. How does the portrayal of these people in this film show some of the limitations of the paradigm through which they are understood?

FILMS RELATED BY GEOGRAPHIC OR SUBJECT AREA:

This film is one of a series on the Yanomamo created out of the Asch/Chagnon partnership. Others include; A Man Called Bee, Magical Death and the Feast. Another film set nearby in Southeastern Columbia and delving more ferociously into the issues of contact and culture change is Disappearing World: The Last of the Cuiva. Also three of John Marshall's African films — N!ai, Meat Fight, and An Argument about a Marriage — deal with socially controlled disputes, the former largely in the context of massive social/cultural change and the latter two wherein the emphasis is kinship obligation.

Distributor: Documentary Educational Resources
Note: See distributor information at the end of the book.

* * * * * * * * * *

# THE BHARVAD PREDICAMENT

Jayasinhji Jhala, director; Roger Sandall, cinematographer
<u>Distributor</u>: Documentary Educational Resources
<u>Format</u>: video only, color, 50 minutes, 1987
<u>Genre</u>: contemporary
<u>Key Words</u>:     Conflict Resolution, Dispute, Ecology — Cultural, India
            — Gujarat, Pastoralism

SUMMARY:

Bharvad cattle herdsmen have been nomadic pastoralists for centuries.
The film presents the conflict that has arisen between the local landholding
farmers and the Bharvad in Dhrangadhra, India. They are in the midst of a
particularly dry season, and competition for the available land and water
resources has escalated producing a state of tension between the farmers
and the herdsmen. The farmers appear to be supported by the government
while the Bharvad are tolerated as a quaint but relatively unimportant
political entity. The history of the relationship between the pastoralists
and the farmers is reviewed in depth and both points of view are
objectively presented. The film clearly demonstrates the influence that
geography, natural resources, and governmental policies have on the
survival of particular ethnic groups and culture.

REASONS FOR ITS USEFULNESS:

As the title suggests, *The Bharvad Predicament* introduces its audience to
the Bharvad of Gujarat and the neighboring Kanbi and Koli farmers who
have been engaged in a long conflict which has recently reached a degree
of seriousness that precludes any easy resolution. Indeed, the film neither
records nor posits a solution to the increasing restrictions placed upon
Bharvad in their attempts to earn a livelihood from cattle herding. Rather,
the film explores the processes — both material and discursive — by
which such conflict emerges, waxes, and wanes. For example, the decision
to interview members of each caste involved in the current dispute
(Bharvad, Kanbi, Koli, and Rajput) makes it evident that both sides have

14

legitimate grievances, and neither side seems more culpable than the other. Moreover, the film reveals that none of the protagonists are free operators; each has vested interests and customary obligations to protect and fulfill of which the type depends upon the individual's location in the caste and mode of production hierarchies. Consequently, the film favors a structural, rather than idiosyncratic, interpretation of the conflict and directs the audience's attention toward larger social forces which influence and often dictate the course of events on the local level. In the end, the spectator is made poignantly aware of the difficulty, if not the impossibility, of achieving a fair and objective resolution to the dispute. To a large extend, this film testifies to the imperfection of the rule of law in societies with clearly delineated hierarchies, be they caste, class, or ethnicity.

## QUESTIONS BEFORE SCREENING:

1. What is a mode of production? Describe the main features of pastoralism.
2. What are patron-client relationships?
3. How does "caste" differ from other sociological categories, such as class and ethnicity?
4. What is cultural ecology? How do anthropologists differ from ecologists in their use of the term "ecology?"
5. What are some of the functions of property laws?

## QUESTIONS AFTER SCREENING:

1. Summarize what occurred when the Forestry Agency introduced the acacia plant in Gujarat. Bear in mind how this affected the livelihood of Bharvad.
2. How did the government's land reform policy of 1947 affect the Bharvad?
3. What means do Bharvad, Kanbi, and Koli have at their disposal to resolve their dispute?
4. How did the recent Land Ceiling Act affect Bharvad?
5. Describe the relationship between Bharvads and Rajputs. Describe the relationship between Kanbi farmers and the government. Compare and contrast these relationships.

FILMS RELATED BY GEOGRAPHIC OR SUBJECT AREA:

A Zenana, by Jayasinhji Jhala and Roger Sandall
Tragada Bhavai, by Jayasinhji Jhala and Roger Sandall

Distributor: Documentary Educational Resources
            Contact: Cynthia Close
Note: See distributor information at the end of the book.

* * * * * * * * * *

---

## - 8 -

## BITTER MELONS

---

John Marshall, filmmaker
Distributor: Documentary Educational Resources
Format: 16mm film, video, color, 30 minutes, 1971
Genre: classic ethnographic film
Key Words:     Southern Africa, !Kung, Ju/Æhoansi, Hunting and
               Gathering, Music, Play

SUMMARY:

This is a film about a small band of /Gwi San. Ten people share a camp,
including a blind musician Ukxone, his wife and son, two older women,
two boys, and another man, !Gai, with his wife and child. Ukxone plays
music that he has composed on his hunting bow: songs in praise of
melons, about trapping antelopes, about shouting and being lost in the
bush. Bitter Melons, his favorite song, is about a woman who learned
from her Bantu neighbors to plant melon seeds. Wild melons taste bitter,
the agriculturalists said. Ukxone's favorite songs evoke the /Gwi
landscape and its diverse wildlife, as well as the routines of daily life:
collecting, hunting, catching a tortoise that is cooked alive and shared.

!Gai, a member of the band, returns one day with a group of his relatives.
Visitors and hosts enjoy the social occasion, as young boys play animal
games (porcupine, hyena) and make their own traditional music on the

16

bow (animal songs, like giraffe and kudu). Men and boys dance the ostrich courting dance." The fluidity of /Gwi bands is revealed when !Gai and his family depart with their other relatives, disappearing into the tall grass of the veld to the sound of Ukxone's Bitter Melons.

## REASONS FOR ITS USEFULNESS:

For centuries, many in the West have believed that the hunting and gathering mode of production is "nasty, brutish, and short." There are also those that, following Rousseau, see "primitive" lifestyles as a romantic way to live. This film tends toward support of the latter interpretation. Having to work only a few hours a day to gain sustenance, the Ju/Æhoansi, at times, have been able to devote more energy to art, music, storytelling, dance, and play. In this film, we hear some wonderful music and see some very interesting forms of play and exercise. We also learn about the ways in which cultural diffusion is introducing horticulture to the band and how this effects music.

## QUESTIONS BEFORE SCREENING:

1.  What are some of the challenges to traditional culture that the Ju/Æhoansi face?
2.  How does music reflect culture?

## QUESTIONS AFTER SCREENING:

1.  What does the film teach us about our nine to five lifestyle?
2.  What can we learn from the film about social organization?

## FILMS RELATED BY GEOGRAPHIC OR SUBJECT AREA:

The Hunters; The Meat Fight; An Argument about a Marriage; A Joking Relationship; N/um Tchai; N!ai, The Story of a !Kung Woman; Pull Ourselves Up or Die Out, all by John Marshall.

Awards: Flaherty Award; CINE Golden Eagle; American Film Festival Blue Ribbon
Reviews: American Anthropologist, Volume 74, Number 4, 1972, pg. 1018-1020, by Alan Lomax;

Landers Reviews, Jan/Feb 1982, pg. 96; Media Digest, April 1980;
New York Times, 10 June 1972, by Howard Thompson.
Associated Reading: The Cinema of John Marshall, edited by Jay Ruby,
Philadelphia: Harwood Academic Publishers, 1993;
The Harmless People, Elizabeth Marshall Thomas, New York: Alfred A.
Knopf, 1959.

Distributor: Documentary Educational Resources
*Note*: See distributor information at the end of the book.

\* \* \* \* \* \* \* \* \* \* \*

---

## - 9 -

## BLACK IS ... BLACK AIN'T

Marlon Riggs, director
Distributor: California Newsreel
Format: video, color, 87 minutes, 1995
Genre: contemporary
Key Words:      African-American Studies, Gender, Homosexuality,
                Identity, Race, Racism, Sexism

SUMMARY:

With *Black Is...Black Ain't*, Riggs focuses attention on the "isms" that
divide and separate, and challenges black people to "reconcile themselves
to each other, to our differences...we have to get over the notion that you
can only be unified as a people as long as everybody agrees. You know we
don't achieve freedom by those means." For centuries American culture
has stereotyped black Americans, but equally devastating have been the
constraining and often contradictory definitions of "blackness" African-
Americans have imposed on each other. The right attire; hair from "conk"
to Afro; ghetto slang or "proper" speech; "true" black religion versus the
false; macho man or superwoman; authentic, Afro-centric or Euro-centric;
sexuality and gender roles: each one of these has been used as a litmus test
in defining the real black man and the true black woman. But is there an

18

essential black identity? Can blackness be reduced to a single acceptable set of experiences that African-Americans should share or even aspire to?

*Black Is...Black Ain't* forcefully confronts the identification of blackness with a hyper-masculinity born of the '60s Black Power Movement. Colorism, the black church, the Civil Rights Movement, family — all continue to be defining factors in today's black communities. *Black Is...Black Ain't* brings it all to the table, knowing, as Riggs says, that "there's a cure for what ails us as a people, and that is for us to talk to each other. We've got to start talking about the ways in which we hurt each other...because nobody can unload the pain or the shame or the guilty not speaking."

Riggs uses his grandmother's gumbo as a metaphor for the rich diversity of black identities. His camera crisscrosses the country bringing us face-to-face with black folks young and old, rich and poor, rural and urban, gay and straight, grappling with the paradox of numerous, often contested, definitions of blackness. Riggs mixes performances by choreographer Bill T. Jones and poet Essex Hemphill and commentary by noted cultural critics Angela Davis, bell hooks, Cornel West, Michele Wallace, Barbara Smith, and Maulana Karenga into this flavorful stew of personal testimony, music, and history.

Riggs' own urgent quest for self-definition and community as a black, gay man dying of AIDS ties the multiple perspectives together. Hooked up to an IV in a hospital bed, Riggs takes strength from his struggle against AIDS from the continual resilience of African-Americans in the face of overwhelming oppression. As his death nears, he conjures up the image of a black community maturing and celebrating the difference and creativity in each one of us.

REASON FOR ITS USEFULNESS:

Black Is...Black Ain't is of value to students of anthropology for a number of reasons. For one, the film reveals the existence of great variation with the social categories it interrogates, and thereby casts doubt upon the empirical neutrality and descriptive accuracy of these analytic categories created by society to organize and regulate itself. Moreover, it drives home the point that identities such as "blackness" and "gayness" are the product of society, not nature, and, consequently, both reflect and shape the values and power structure of the society in which they are conceived. In other words, identities are simultaneously ascribed to groups and projected by them. This recognition of the role that individuals and groups play in the construction of their own self-image is particularly important, for it directs the audience's attention to the essentially political character of bearing and conferring particular identities. As agents possessing the will and the means to counteract existing representations with ones of their own making, they engage in a discursive act that may eventually result in the affirmation of the self as well as the improvement of the group's overall socio-economic status. Yet, the film also makes clear that a group's attempt to define itself may just as easily unleash the forces of repression and fragmentation if it fails to embrace the diversity intrinsic to the whole. While the film does not address directly the paradox of boundless communities, Riggs message rings out poignantly: if unity is strength, then unity must be built upon the broadest social base possible.

QUESTIONS BEFORE SCREENING:

1. What is the significance of a name?·
2. Name several kinds of identities which are integrally bound up with one's sense of self.
3. How and why are linguistic dialects created and perpetuated?
4. Who is considered to be black in the United States, and upon what criteria is this classification made?
5. Who are considered to be white in the united States? Why is white racial identity often more important than white ethnic identity?

QUESTIONS AFTER SCREENING:

1. Why does Riggs imply that disagreement within a community is much better than a false consensus?
2. Summarize the argument in the film that says that the Black Power Movement in the '60s focused, in large part, upon the black, heterosexual men, excluding to a large extent black women and black, gay men?
3. Why is it difficult for many black feminists to criticize the behavior of some black men?
4. According to Riggs, why is silence harmful?

5. What is the significance of knowing the history of one's people and country?

FILMS RELATED BY GEOGRAPHIC OR SUBJECT AREA:

Color Adjustment, by Marion Riggs, distributed by California Newsreel;
Ethnic Notions, by Marion Riggs, distributed by California Newsreel;
Brincando El Charco, by Frances Negron-Muntaner

Distributor: California Newsreel
Note: See distributor information at the end of the book.

* * * * * * * * * * *

---

## - 10 -

## BLACK HARVEST
---

Bob Connolly and Robin Anderson, filmmakers
Distributor: contact Documentary Educational Resources for latest information
Format: video, color, 62 minutes, 1990
Genre: classic ethnographic film
Key Words: Papua New Guinea, Irian Jaya

SUMMARY:

This is the third in a series of films including *First Contact* and *Joe Leahy's Neighbors*, dealing with cultural change in highland New Guinea. It puts the economic situation into sharp focus as it follows a labor dispute surrounding one of Joe Leahy's farms. Leahy hired dozens of his economically marginalized neighbors to clear forest and plant coffee. When international coffee prices dropped, Leahy couldn't pay his workers. Anger and frustration exacerbate tensions in the community, many turn to traditional patterns of ritual warfare and try to exact revenge on Leahy. Connolly and Anderson negotiate difficult relationships as they try to show both sides of the story.

## REASONS FOR ITS USEFULNESS:

This film is best shown in conjunction with the first two in the series. Depicting economic conflict and cultural change, it is useful for those interested in economic development in the Third World. Entrepreneurial activity at the fringes of the World agricultural market are shown to be quite fragile enterprises. Not only are they effected by the vagaries of world pricing systems but they are also impacted by local histories and local cultural conflicts. The filmmakers succeed in portraying these issues even though they face many difficulties.

## QUESTIONS BEFORE SCREENING:

1. How has labor been traditionally organized in Papua New Guinea?
2. What changes occur in social organization when capitalism is introduced?

## QUESTIONS AFTER SCREENING:

1. Who has the most valid case — Joe Leahy or his employees — and why?
2. Should labor laws incorporate traditional values and how?

## FILMS RELATED BY GEOGRAPHIC OR SUBJECT AREA:

Dead Birds, Tidikawa and Friends, First Contact, Joe Leahy's Neighbors

Distributor: Documentary Educational Resources
*Note*: See distributor information at the end of the book.

\* \* \* \* \* \* \* \* \* \*

# BRINCANDO EL CHARCO

Frances Negron-Muntaner, director
<u>Distributor</u>: Independent Television Service
<u>Format</u>: video, color, 1994
<u>Genre</u>: experimental
<u>Key Words</u>:      Bi-culturalism, Homosexuality, Identity, Immigration,
                  Latinas, Puerto Rico, United States

SUMMARY:

Frances Negron-Muntaner's film, *Brincando el Charco*, is a semi-autobiographical film which takes as its subject matter the complexities and contradictions inherent in being Puerto Rican in the United States, particularly when one is homosexual. As Negron-Muntaner puts it, "one is a minority within a minority" and, therefore, highly marginal to the dominant society. However, in the case of Claudia, *Brincando el Charco*'s fictional character, she finds herself uncomfortably caught between two cultures (native and adoptive) and feels truly at home in neither. Through a clever blend of documentary and scripted scenes, the audience follows the protagonist through her effort to deal with the breech between past and present, and the "there" (Puerto Rico and her family) with the "here" (the United States, her lover, and her career). The catalyst for this internal dialogue is a phone call that Claudia receives from her brother in Puerto Rico, informing her that their father has recently died. This throws Claudia into a tumult of ambivalent and painful emotions, because she and her father had been estranged since he threw her out of the house at the age of sixteen upon learning of her sexual preference. Forced to make a decision about whether or not to return "home" for the funeral, she is confronted with the need to reconcile these two worlds. She finds an important channel for the ensuing onslaught of emotions and thoughts in her photography — an element of the film that is ironically reflexive.

## REASONS FOR ITS USEFULNESS:

*Brincando el Charco* is important as an anthropological film for its attention to such cultural issues as racism, homophobia, linguistic discrimination, bi-culturalism, and hegemony. However, what makes this film differ from others with similar topical orientations is that *Brincando el Charco* addresses these issues from the perspective of a fictional character modeled after the filmmaker. Negron-Muntaner's decision to use scripted scenes in a film that has the feel of a documentary complements her phenomenological approach to the subjects mentioned above and, consequently, enables the film to be as emotionally and psychologically compelling while still being intellectually satisfying. As the film unfolds, the audience is drawn into Claudia's personal drama in which she explores her feelings of exile and displacement.

## QUESTIONS BEFORE SCREENING:

1. What is (cultural) hegemony?
2. What is the current political relationship between the United States and Puerto Rico?
3. To what do the terms "bi-culturalism" and "multi culturalism" refer?
4. To what extend do you think memory shapes one's sense of identity?
5. What are "diglossia" and "code-switching," and in what kind of situations are they most likely to exist/be practiced?

## QUESTIONS AFTER SCREENING:

1. How do perceptions of race in Puerto Rico differ from perceptions of race in the United States?
2. How does Claudia respond to the fact the gay pride parade in Puerto Rico was organized by men from the United States?
3. Discuss the meanings of "home" for Claudia. Where does it exist for her?
4. Discuss the relationship between language and culture.
5. Discuss the film's structure in relation to its content.

FILMS RELATED BY GEOGRAPHIC OR SUBJECT AREA:

Black Is...Black Ain't, by Marlon Riggs
Pocho Novella, by Coco Fusco

Distributor: Independent Television Service
*Note*: See distributor information at the end of the book.

\* \* \* \* \* \* \* \* \* \* \*

## - 12 -

## CANNIBAL TOURS

Dennis O'Rourke, producer/director
Distributor: Direct Cinema Limited
Format: 1/2 VHS, color, 77 minutes, 1987
Genre: contemporary
Key Words:     Cannibalism, Tourism, Primitive, Global Economy,
                Culture Contact, Authenticity

SUMMARY:

*Cannibal Tours* is a collection of disarming and revealing moments.
Western tourists bargain for artifacts, pay cash to watch tribal rituals,
visit former sacred sites, and give their interpretation of Papua New
Guinea culture. The tribespeople in turn comment on the strangeness of
the whites who visit with unimaginable amounts of money and part with it
only reluctantly. This gently ironic film neither condones or condemns the
tourist or the Papua New Guineans. It offers a series of striking
observations that exemplify both the quandary of culture clash and the
human sameness of people everywhere.

REASONS FOR ITS USEFULNESS:

This film uses sensational appeal to engage the audience, then twists it
back on the viewer, ambushing them with a glimpse in the mirror. For
viewers this film is sometimes disturbing, sometimes startling, but always

gets them thinking. The "cannibals" subtitled observations about the tourists for whom they perform "the primitive" are insightful and serve to alert viewers to the intelligence and similar concerns; e.g., paying for school and clothing for the kids, of those who may appear quite different from us. They also serve as a foil to the tourists comments about them "vegetating in nature" and the need to bring them "civilization." The colonial era photos and Mozart musical accompaniment attest to how civilization was brought, while personal testimony gives the viewer a taste of what changes were wrought. The film often startles viewers enough to get them to reconsider ingrained "folk knowledge" equating physical evolution with cultural form. The film's focus upon exchange relationships wherein indigenous people seem to be almost desperate to get money though they do not seem to fully grasp how it works and why they seem to get the proverbial "short end," along with juxtapositions such as the tourist yacht and wooden canoes, or the BBC World Service News against open expanses of the South Pacific are great contextual motors to initiate discussions of the global economy and where indigenous groups fit into it.

## QUESTIONS BEFORE SCREENING:

1. What is cannibalism? Do we practice it? Under what conditions is it acceptable?
2. Why is cannibalism considered primitive? Are people cannibals because they cannot get enough to eat? What are other reasons for it? What is the Eucharist/
3. What is the global economy? Is there a hierarchy of economic power involved in it?
4. What is colonialism? What effects does it have on indigenous groups?
5. What is authenticity? What is an authentic recreation? What is the difference between a stereotypical event and an authentic event?

## QUESTIONS AFTER SCREENING:

1. What do the tourists think of the Sepik people? What era — what point in time — do the tourists think they are in? Do they seem "primitive?"
2. What do the Sepik people think of the tourists? Why do they continue to interact with the tourists given their frustrations?

3. Do the Sepik peoples seem to be performing for the tourists? How do they dress; what do they do when the tourists are about? Is it authentic? How is it different when the tourists are not about?
4. Is there a relationship drawn between tourism and colonialism? How are they similar and different?
5. What do you think the filmmaker's main point is? Who are the cannibals?

Distributor: Direct Cinema Limited
*Note*: See distributor information at the end of the book.

* * * * * * * * * * *

---

## - 13 -

## CHRONICLE OF A SUMMER

Jean Rouch (filmmaker), with Edgar Morin
Distributor: contact Documentary Educational Resources for latest information
Format: 16mm film, video, black and white, 75 minutes, 1960
Genre: classic ethnographic film
Key Words: France, Paris, Cinema Verite, Algeria

SUMMARY:

A film experiment in Parisian sociology or a sociological inquiry into Paris. This film, produced in collaboration with Edgar Morin, is an attempt at cinematographic investigation using an entirely new technique of synchronous sound (direct cinema) on young French people in the summer of 1960: a moment when it was thought that the war in Algeria was going to end, but when it was prolonged, and when the incidents in the Congo added the problems of independence in the African states to the problems of the Maghreb states. The film follows during several months — both the investigation itself and the evolution of the principle characters: Marcelline (former deportee) doing socio-economic research; her friend Jean-Pierre, a student of philosophy; Marie-Lou, of Italian origin, a secretary at Cahiers du Cinema; Angelo and his friend Jacques, workers at Renault; an SNCF employee; discouraged former militant and his wife; Landry, a student from the Ivory Coast coming from high school in Villeneuve sur Lot. Around this group we discover other Parisians, unknown people met in the streets: Nadine, high school friend of Landry; Raymond, a student from Ivory Coast at a commercial school; a happy artist-painter couple; a cover girl; a saleswoman in a fashion ship; the daughters of Edgar Morin; and the two authors of the film.

## REASONS FOR ITS USEFULNESS:

At the beginning, the question asked is "How do you live?" but essential questions quickly appear: political despair, solitude, the battle against boredom. Vacation arrives, the factories empty, the beaches fill up. Algeria will be for some other year. All of the protagonists attend the first screening of the film. They discuss, accept or reject it. The two authors find themselves alone in the face of this cruel but fascinating experiment in cinema verite.

This film represents a major leap forward for documentary and ethnographic film. Not only are the makers of the film portrayed, but the investigation itself becomes a character in the film. Covering a wide range of topics from the Holocaust to fashion, from politics to emotional intimacy, the film is a provocative portrait of Paris in 1960. The film is useful in that it raises interesting questions about consciousness, emotion, memory, politics, and the ethnographic project. It also can lead to fruitful discussion about the ethics of image-making.

## QUESTIONS BEFORE SCREENING:

1. How should an investigator go about conducting an ethnography of an industrial city?
2. What is the role of the investigator in instigating the situations that occur in front of a camera?

## QUESTIONS AFTER SCREENING:

1. What is the role of memory in day-to-day life?
2. What do Rouch and Morin contribute to a discussion about representation?

Awards: Festival Prizes, Cannes, Venice, Mannheim, 1961.
Reviews: Visual Anthropology, vol. 2, 1989.
Associated Reading: The Cinematic Griot: the Ethnography of Jean
Rouch, by Paul Stoller, Chicago: The University of Chicago Press, 1992.

Distributor: Documentary Educational Resources
*Note*: See distributor information at the end of the book.

\* \* \* \* \* \* \* \* \* \* \*

## - 14 -

## COLOR ADJUSTMENT

Marlon Riggs, director; Ruby Dee, narrator
Distributor: California Newsreel
Format: video only, rental, color, 87 minutes, 1991
Genre: contemporary
Key Words:    African-American History and Culture, Racism,
                Representation, Television

SUMMARY:

The video traces forty years of race relations and the portrayal of the
black American through the lens of prime-time television programming.
From "Amos and Andy" to "The Cosby Show," from interviews with
black actors to Hollywood producers, and with scholarly commentary, the
turbulent story of the integration of prime-time television unfolds.

REASONS FOR ITS USEFULNESS:

In many respects, *Color Adjustment* is not so much an exploration of the
attributes or circumstances of a specific ethnic or social group as it is a
critical inquiry into television's representation of African-Americans since
the inception of the medium. While this brief description might sound like
the film would be of greater interest to historians or media scholars, it
would be an egregious mistake for anthropologists to overlook this film in
their search for new pedagogical materials and sources of intellectual

stimulation — for a number of different reasons. First, *Color Adjustment* examines the problems inherent in the act of representation and, thus, addresses an issue of major concern for anthropologists working in the current intellectual and political climate. Second, the director's choice to view the televised portrayal of African-Americans over a relatively long historical period throws into critical relief the dynamic relationship between society and its representations, and, consequently, *Color Adjustment* underscores the methodological and theoretical importance of making time depth an integral part of all studies involving cultural phenomena. Third, the film testifies to the role of dominant ideologies and discourses in shaping the content of TV programs which are often presupposed by their audiences to be value-free and politically neutral forms of entertainment. Finally, *Color Adjustment* can be said to be of relevance to anthropology in that it is a critical interrogation of an industry that has a tremendous influence over an extremely large and diverse percentage of the world's population, and this project can be seen as operating in tandem with the current trend in anthropology to study not just the effects of power (oppression and cultural homogenization) but the structures through which power is exercised.

QUESTIONS BEFORE SCREENING:

1. What is a representation? What is its relationship to that which it represents?
2. To what extend is the media an instrument of ideology? Whose ideology?
3. Is it important to see oneself or one's community portrayed in the media? Why or why not?
4. Does the media have any obligation to be socially relevant or responsible? Why or why not?
5. What is the "American Dream?" How has this dream changed throughout time?

QUESTIONS AFTER SCREENING:

1. Discuss the meaning of the title *Color Adjustment*.
2. What is the relationship between advertising and the media?
3. Discuss the functions of humor in TV as understood by those interviewed by Riggs.

4. According to the film, are "positive" representations of a community always positive? Are "negative" representations of a community always negative/ Why or why not?
5. Is narrow casting a possible solution to some of the diversity problems associated with the media, particularly TV?

FILMS RELATED BY GEOGRAPHIC OR SUBJECT AREA:

Imagining Indians, by Victor Masayesva
Ethnic Notions, by Marlon Riggs

Distributor: California Newsreel
*Note*: See distributor information at the end of the book.

* * * * * * * * * * *

## - 15 -

## DEAD BIRDS

Robert Gardner, producer/director
Distributor: C.R.M.P.
Format: 16mm, 1/2 VHS, color, 83 minutes, 1963
Genre: classic
Key Words:     Agriculturalists, Ritual Warfare, Colonialism, Filmic Structure

SUMMARY:

An ethnographic cross-section of the life and customs of the Dani people of the Baliem Valley in western New Guinea. Explores the nature of primitive warfare and its motivations. Sponsored by the Peabody Museum at Harvard University.

REASONS FOR ITS USEFULNESS:

This film is a classic documentary style, voice-over narrative film which uses several fiction film techniques to carry its message. Students viewing this film can easily fall into a typical receptive state of "half-death," ingesting the disembodied narration and easily fitting the images they see into preconditioned categories of noble savage or simply savage. It is important, therefore, to challenge them to view the film carefully as a particular arrangement of bits of sound and pictures put together from over a year's worth of field recording. Some reading, such as excerpts from Carl Heider's The Dani of West Irian: An Ethnographic Companion to Dead Birds and/or Jay Ruby's An Anthropological Critique of the Films of Robert Gardner in Journal of Film and Video, 43 (4), pp. 3-17, helps to prepare students so they can form their own opinions upon viewing. If the audience is properly prepared, this is a great film with which to begin to deconstruct many simple stereotypes of indigenous people; e.g., violent, simple, a part of nature, as well as narratives from our culture which perpetuate them.

QUESTIONS BEFORE VIEWING:

1. What are common stereotypes of peoples labeled primitive or savage?
2. Do we believe in ghosts? Do we believe in the actions of forces that we cannot directly sense?
3. Why do people fight wars? What is ritualized warfare? Do we practice it?
4. How are documentary films different from fiction films? What intentions and techniques do they share and what ones are different?
5. What is an ethnographic film? How are they made? Who makes them.

QUESTIONS AFTER VIEWING:

1. How do we learn information about the Dani in the film? Do the subjects of the film speak? Do they seem to understand that they are being filmed?
2. Does the narrator tell us things he cannot possibly know? How does the narrator know what Pu-ah is thinking? How does he know that Wae-ak's wife knows her husband has reached his guard tower?
3. Why would the filmmaker make it appear that the battles in the film occur one after the other? Were there any indications that they did not? Did the audio and visual tracks seem to match up?
4. Does the film cast the Dani as violent? Reflecting on our own history, do they seem more or less violent than us? What similarities and

differences do you perceive between us and them in warfare?
5.  Does the film explain the cause of all the fighting? Why does the film leave out the history of the region? Could historical factors such as colonialism be tied to the violence?
6.  What do we learn of Dani religion and beliefs? Who in our culture is afraid of ghosts?

Distributor: C.R.M. Films
*Note*: See distributor information at the end of the book.

* * * * * * * * * * *

# DIGGING FOR SLAVES: THE EXCAVATION OF AMERICAN SLAVE SITES

Jonathan Dent, producer for the BBC
Distributor: Films for the Humanities, Inc.
Format: 1/2 VHS, color, 50 minutes, 1992
Genre: contemporary
Key Words:     Archaeology, Artifact, Slavery, History, Myth, Representation, Race

SUMMARY:

This program provides many fascinating and surprising details at excavations of eighteenth century slave quarters on Middleburg Plantation near Charleston; at Monticello, the home of Thomas Jefferson, whose slave holdings seem so irreconcilable with his expressed views on human freedom; and at Colonial Williamsburg, which until recently neglected to show the lives of the slaves, who made up over half the town's population.

REASONS FOR ITS USEFULNESS:

Slavery is a topic that most Americans would rather forget. In terms of history the reality is slaves are, for the most part, forgotten. They live on in cultural myths if at all. *Digging for Slaves* shows some archaeologists who are in fact interested in the lives and lifeways of the United State's hardest working early pioneers. Through a discussion of findings at various field sites, archaeologists demonstrate the ingenuity, loyalty, perseverance, perspicacity, and enormous accomplishments of slaves in the founding days of the nation. The conundrum of owning people while holding principles of liberty and equality is raised historically for Jefferson and discussed in the context of attempts to reconstruct many aspects of slaves' lives. The film touches on the difficulties of discussing such a sensitive topic currently through the voice of an African-American interpretive guide at Williamsburg. The artifacts make the archaeologist's points about the realities of slaves' lives. They also point to the shadowy existence we have come to accept as some people's past while assuming a colorful, detailed history exists for others. The film, thus, makes the work of archaeology more real and provides a variety of types of actual archaeological work to counter the Indiana Jones syndrome.

QUESTIONS BEFORE SCREENING:

1.  What is slavery? How was slavery in the United States different than slavery in other places, at other times?
2.  What was its basis or justification? Its legal basis valued what rights over what others?
3.  Who were made slaves? Who were owners?
4.  What do archaeologists study? How is that different from what historians study?
5.  What is an artifact/ How do artifacts relate to culture?

QUESTIONS AFTER SCREENING:

1.  Did you learn any new facts about slaves that you did not know before? What?
2.  Have you studied United States history? Did you already know about many of the things discussed in the film? Why not? To whom are they important?
3.  How can the archaeologists know so much about how the slaves lived?
4.  What were important artifacts in the film? What did the archaeologists use these artifacts for? (How were the artifacts used by the archaeologists?)

5. Name several different kinds of archaeologists or archaeological practices you saw in the film.

Distributor: Films for the Humanities, Inc.
*Note*: See distributor information at the end of the book.

\* \* \* \* \* \* \* \* \* \* \*

---

**- 17 -**

## DIVINE HORSEMEN: LIVING GODS OF HAITI

Maya Deeren, filmmaker
Distributor: Mystic Fire Video
Format: video only, black and white, 60 minutes, 1985
Genre: classic
Key Words:    Diaspora-African, Haiti, Polytheism, Possession, Religion-Vodoun, Ritual

SUMMARY:

Maya Deren takes us on a journey into the fascinating world of the Vodoun religion, whose devotees commune with the cosmic powers through invocation, offerings, song, and dance. The Vodoun pantheon of deities, or Lao, are witnessed as living gods and goddesses, actually taking possession of their devotees. The soundtrack conveys the incantatory power of the ritual drumming and singing.

REASONS FOR ITS USEFULNESS;

*Divine Horsemen* is a beautifully shot and highly respectful film that offers its audience insight into Haitian Vodoun. It is a film that could be appreciated by a wide range of people, including those with a serious interest in anthropology. For one, it shows the richness and diversity that is Vodoun. For another, it helps to discredit and dispel many of the negative and simplistic stereotypes of Vodoun that exist in the United States and elsewhere. Rather than interviewing people on camera about their practices and beliefs, *Divine Horsemen* is mainly an observational film which focuses solely upon the ceremonies conducted in honor and invocation of the large body of Vodoun deities. Unlike some observational films, Deren's camera rarely seems invasive; rather it seems to be part of the events it records and treats its subjects with dignity. Moreover she applies previous experiments with filmic time to the making of *Divine Horsemen* by shooting possessions in slow motion. This has the effect, both literally and figuratively, of setting the possessions in relief against other parts of the ceremonies. Like Jean Rouch, Deren's camera attempts to convey that which does not lend itself to visible representation — emotional and psychological states. However, this is not to say that *Divine Horsemen* substitutes evocation for description. On the contrary, it shows the sequence of events that constitute a Vodoun ceremony, beginning with the drawing of ritual icons on the ground in chalk. Through the intermittent voice of the off screen narrator, the audience learns that these drawings are not merely decorative, but, more importantly, instrumental in achieving communication between the spirit world and mortal human beings. These drawings do not merely represent an idea; they embody it and give it existence. Moreover, the audience learns that, unlike members of wealthier and more institutionalized religions, Vodoun adherents build their "church" anew for each ceremony, thus requiring more active participation on the part of Vodoun congregations. Upon the iconic representation of the crossroads (where divine and mortal meet), a pole is erected and food offerings and libations are placed around it. The audience learns that these offerings are not propitiations to the divinities, but enticements for the divinities to manifest themselves by entering and possessing human hosts. According to Vodoun, food is viewed as a life giving force necessary for human as well as divine strength, and animal sacrifices are considered an important element in increasing the power of divinities. Moreover, the audience learns that Vodoun initiates do not perceive sacrifice as the taking of life, but rather the transferal of life. There are many other reasons for recommending *Divine Horsemen* to anthropologists — such as the syncretic nature of Vodoun, its connection to African religions, etc... — however, suffice it to say, this film is not merely of heuristic value to students of anthropology, it is a pleasure to watch for its own sake.

QUESTIONS BEFORE SCREENING:

1. What is syncretism?

2. What is the relationship between the sacred and the secular?
3. What are the features of a religious congregation?
4. What is polytheism?
5. What are the characteristics of ritual in anthropological terms?

QUESTIONS AFTER SCREENING:

1. How has Vodoun been shaped by major historical events?
2. What occurs during possession by the Loas? What is its purpose?
3. Discuss the creative dimensions of Vodoun.
4. What is the role of music and dance in Vodoun ceremonies?
5. What is the purpose of carnival in Haiti? How does it compare to other carnivals, such as the Mardi Gras carnival in New Orleans?

Distributor; Mystic Fire Video
*Note*: See distributor information at the end of the book.

* * * * * * * * * *

- 18 -

## FAMILIAR PLACES

David and Judith MacDougall, filmmakers
Distributor: contact Documentary Educational Resources for latest information
Format: 16mm film, video, color, 50 minutes, 1980
Genre: classic ethnographic film
Key Words: Australia, Aboriginals, Land Rights, The Dreamtime

SUMMARY:

The film follows the mapping of traditional clan territory in compliance with the Australian Aboriginal Land Rights Act. A young anthropologist, the filmmakers, and an extended aboriginal family spend several weeks in the Northern Australian bush recording the names of places that were once the areas in which ancient clan rituals and living took place. First, a ritual takes place where the clan matron introduces her children to the local dreamtime spirits for the first time and asks for their protection. She extends this courtesy to the filmmakers, as well. The film follows the clan elders as they discuss local terrain and the ancient stories that are attached. Natural springs, highly charged sites, were once very secret ritual locations; the filmmakers are present at the discovery of a new one. The clan elders have to decide how much they can reveal of their local knowledge without violating traditional secrecy laws and still comply with the Australian law and the anthropologist's need for information. A visit to a site of ritual warfare and a site where victims of disease brought by the West were cremated is a particularly charged scene.

REASONS FOR ITS USEFULNESS:

Not only is this film a good introduction to aboriginal traditions, but it also introduces viewers to contemporary issues surrounding the interaction of indigenous and national law. The two legal systems are fundamentally opposed in some respects. One system requires secrecy; the other requires disclosure. To comply with Australian law, aborigines are required to put their own law in jeopardy. Negotiating what to tell and what not to tell is a process that many aboriginal groups have had to undergo as they try to claim traditional lands. This film follows one such story and also follows the emotional journey as the older generation remembers their youth.

QUESTIONS BEFORE SCREENING:

1. What is the nature of traditional Australian aboriginal law?
2. How does this legal system differ from the West's in relation to property law?

QUESTIONS AFTER SCREENING:

1. What do we learn about cultural survival from the film?
2. What are some of the ethical issues of a film like this?

FILMS RELATED BY GEOGRAPHIC OR SUBJECT AREA:

Three Horsemen; Goodbye Old Man; Two Laws

Associated Reading: Bad Aboriginal Art, by Eric Michaels, Minneapolis: University of Minnesota Press, 1994.

Distributor: Documentary Educational Resources
*Note*: See distributor information at the end of the book.

\* \* \* \* \* \* \* \* \* \*

---

## - 19 -

## FIRST CONTACT

Bob Conolly and Robin Anderson, filmmakers
Distributor: Documentary Educational Resources
Format: video, color, 54 minutes, 1983
Genre: classic ethnographic film
Key Words: Papua New Guinea, Irian Jaya

SUMMARY:

In the 1930s, Australian miners lead by Michael Leahy and his brothers made their first trek into the New Guinea highlands. This was the first contact between white people and highlanders. Compelling footage of the initial meetings is combined with interviews of the surviving brothers and highlanders who recall the impressions and shock of those long ago events. The film is ironic, poignant, and often chilling. It's ironic to see recent shots of the natives, once so isolated, sporting Western clothes and chuckling over old photos of themselves. It's poignant to hear women recall being sexually "sold" to the visitors despite their fears. It's chilling to hear the Leahy brothers matter-of-factly explain why they killed their less hospitable hosts, forgetting that, whatever the danger may have been, no invitation had been proffered them in the first place. It's a disturbing film, full of head-on challenges to colonial and racist attitudes. Yet it's a deeply human experience, too: Its message, strongly implied if not stated, is that some kind of rapport is bound to develop in any situation, however clouded the circumstances may be by isolation, ignorance, and the urge for domination.

## REASONS FOR ITS USEFULNESS:

Most cultures living in relative isolation were invaded by the West in the past few centuries. Parts of Papua New Guinea came late in this process, being invaded for the first time in only the last 50 years. Not many of these first contacts were filmed. This film uses historical footage and recollections of witnesses to tell the story of greed and exploitation. While the film may be shocking at times, it is also an important historical document, dealing with cultural change in a path-breaking fashion.

## QUESTIONS BEFORE SCREENING:

1. Why have Westerners for centuries invaded other people's territories?
2. How is power exercised when two cultures come into contact?

## QUESTIONS AFTER SCREENING:

1. What do we learn about cultural survival from the film?
2. What are some of the ethical issues of a film like this?

## FILMS RELATED BY GEOGRAPHIC OR SUBJECT AREA:

Dead Birds; Tidikawa and Friends; Joe Leahy's Neighbors; Black Harvest

Awards: Academy Award Nominee; Festival dei Popoli, Florence, Italy, First Prize; Cinema du Reel, Paris, Grand Prix; Sydney Film Festival, Best Documentary; Australian Film Institute Awards, Best Feature Documentary; Silver Sesterce, Nyon; San Francisco Film Festival, First Prize in Sociology; American Film Festival Red Ribbon; Australian Teachers of Media, Best Documentary

Distributor: Documentary Educational Resources
*Note*: See distributor information at the end of the book.

\* \* \* \* \* \* \* \* \* \*

# IMAGINING INDIANS

Victor Masayesva, producer/director
Distributor: Documentary Educational Resources
Format: 1/2 VHS, color, 56 minutes, 1992
Genre: indigenous film, contemporary
Key Words:     Indian, Stereotype, Exploitation, Representation, Tribe,
Nation, State

SUMMARY:

This Hopi filmmaker presents a Native perspective on the
misrepresentation of Native Americans in feature films. Masayesva
breaks with strict documentary conventions and feels free to use a
combination of scripted scenes, documentary and feature archival footage,
and interviews. Weaving a complex narrative, he plumbs the ways in
which Native Americans react to, attempt to work with, or overtly resist
their representation by the dominant White culture. We get an eye-opening
look at recent popular films by Kevin Costner and Robert Redford.
Intercut through all this is a subtheme about how a romanticized "noble
savage" view of American Indians has gone hand-in-hand with the
commodification (commercialism) and appropriation of their arts and
material culture.

REASONS FOR ITS USEFULNESS:

Many people are still confused about who the people gathered under the
label Indian are. Through this film, Victor Masayesva initiates contact
with a range of Indigenous People, contrasting the different personalities
and points of view of "real Indians" with The Indian created by
Hollywood. Not at all a standard "scientific" type documentary or
ethnographic film, it uses a variety of filmic techniques to make its point
regarding the relationship of the dominant culture with Indians. It reflects
in inversion, and thus questions, the basis of most people's knowledge
about Indians by weaving real stories, melodrama, a variety of visual
effects, and mesmerizing indigenous music, dancing, and singing. These

latter elements also serve to convey to the viewer a sense of a some "other" (nonintellectual) sacred power, a common thread of North American Indian belief, in a direct, unromanticized, nonacademic fashion. By attempting to shake off imposed categories, such as science or Indian or tribe, the film opens viewers to consider Indians as peoples and Nations. It also carries the exploitation of Indians, something frequently assumed to be a historical legacy, into the present.

QUESTIONS BEFORE SCREENING:

1. Why do we call the indigenous inhabitants of the Americas Indians? What does indigenous mean?
2. If we call them by one name, are they all the same? What differences exist/existed between different groups?
3. Where does the name tribe come from? What did different Indian groups call themselves? Is that what we call them?
4. What is the difference between a tribe and a nation? A Nation and a State?
5. When you think of Indians, what do you think of? Where did these ideas come from?
6. Why were so many of them killed? What happened to their land, rights, and political power?

QUESTIONS AFTER SCREENING:

1. Do the Indians in the film all have similar points of view? What are their differences? What do they share?
2. In what ways does Hollywood stereotype Indian people? How has this changed over time? How do the Indians in the film appear different from those in the Hollywood films?
3. Why do you think the scene in the dentist's office is so prominent in the film?
4. Do the Indians in the film seem to have control over the use of their own culture?
5. How is music and signing used in the film? What effect does it have on you? Do you think your reaction was the filmmaker's intention?
6. Is this film a documentary? Is it fiction? Why do you think techniques associated with fiction films are used?

Distributor: Documentary Educational Resources
*Note*: See distributor information at the end of the book.

\* \* \* \* \* \* \* \* \* \*

# IN AND OUT OF AFRICA

Lucien Taylor, director; Ilisa Barbash, producer
Distributor: University of California Extension Media Center (UCEMC)
Format: video, rental, color, 59 minutes, 1993
Genre: contemporary
Key Words:    African Art, African Studies, Art Collectors, Economic
           Trade, French Language, Nigeria

## SUMMARY:

Explores with irony and humor the issues of authenticity, taste, culture, and racial politics in the multimillion-dollar transnational African art trade. Interweaves stories of Western collectors, Muslim traders, African artists, and intellectuals, as well as stories of the filmmakers themselves to focus on Nigerian art dealer Gabai Baare, showing how he adds economic value to and changes the "meaning" of the wood pieces he sells by interpreting and mediating between the cultural values of African artists and Western consumers.

## REASONS FOR ITS USEFULNESS:

*In and Out of Africa* is an interesting and humorous film that focuses primarily upon exploring the meaning of art. It does this through viewing it within a cross-cultural context; namely, that provided by the international trade in West African sculptures. Through the story of Gabai Baare, a Muslim Hausa trader who sells abroad, the audience learns that art has nearly as many meanings as there are people to provide definitions. However, this does not mean that discourses on art are primarily personal or aesthetic in nature. Rather, the audience learns that people's attitudes toward art and their criteria for what constitutes art are culturally relative.

In addition to discrediting the notion of "Art," *In and Out of Africa* interrogates the ways in which value is ascribed to the art object. Although the film reveals that the market plays an important role in determining the price of a wood sculpture, it also testifies to the role of taste in establishing the monetary value of an objet d'art. West Africans have learned through decades of trading that Americans, in particular, desire antique sculptures over reproductions and are willing to pay considerably more for them. Many sculptors and traders have capitalized on this preference by engaging in the production of "fake antiques." Of relevance for the anthropologist is not that some West Africans have duped incautious Americans into believing they have bought cultural relics (although this is certainly interesting), but that Americans and Europeans place such emphasis on the categories of "authentic" and "fake." As several people interviewed in the film argue — how can such a singular quality so affect an object's intrinsic value? Finally, the film calls into question "art" as a universal category, especially when art is meant to be both secular and nonfunctional.

QUESTIONS BEFORE SCREENING:

1. What is art? How does one define it? Is there a difference between art and craft; between fine art and folk art?
2. What is the purpose of trade? What motivates trade, and what are some of its consequences?
3. What is meant by the phrase "free market?"
4. What is an oral tradition, and how does sit relate to literacy?
5. What does the term "value added" mean?

QUESTIONS AFTER SCREENING:

1. Explain why sculptures of colonials are popular among both Euro-Americans and West African sculptors.
2. Who are the art traders in this film? How do they relate to both foreign buyers and the producers of the sculptures? Why are the traders needed as intermediaries?
3. Describe the significance of wooden sculptures and masks to West African sculptors, on the one hand, and Muslim traders and Euro-American buyers, on the other.
4. Why does Gabai Baare state that he doesn't like to trade in wood; that

he only does it because he needs the money?
5.  Why do people go to great lengths to age the appearance of West African sculptures?

FILMS RELATED BY GEOGRAPHIC OR SUBJECT AREA:

Australia's Art of the Dreamtime: Quinkin County, by WIPB-TV
Australia; Whose Paintings? Jayasinhji Jhala and Lindsey Powell, D.E.R.

Distributor: University of California Media Extension Center
*Note*: See distributor information at the end of the book.

\* \* \* \* \* \* \* \* \* \* \*

---

## - 22 -

## INCIDENTS OF TRAVEL IN CHICHEN ITZA

Quetzil Castaneda, director; Jeffrey Himpele, cameraman
Distributor: Documentary Educational Resources
Format: video, rental or sale, color, 90 minutes, 1997
Genre: contemporary, reflexive
Key Words:      Archeological Sites - Chichen Itza, Native Americans -
                Maya, Mexico, New Age Religions, Rituals, Tourism

SUMMARY:

This original ethnographic video depicts how New Agers, the Mexican state, tourists, and 1920's archaeologists all contend to "clear" the site of the antique Maya city of Chichen Itza in order to produce their own idealized and unobstructed visions of "Maya" while the local Maya themselves struggle to occupy the site as vendors and artisans. The setting is the spring Equinox when a shadow said to represent the Maya serpent-god Kukulkan appear on one temple pyramid. As more than 40,000 New Age spiritualists and secular tourists from the United States and Mexico converge to witness this solar phenomenon, the video depicts the surrounding social event as a complicated entanglement of expected dualisms concerning tourism. Going beyond previous films that reduce tourism to neo-colonial and exoticizing social relations, this video portrays a Maya cultural site where U.S. New Agers — rather than local Mayas — appear as exotic ritualists who are on display for other secular tourists and for local Mayas. While the video does examine representations of Mayas by visiting New Agers as part of globalizing discourses on the exotic and evolution, it also shows how, during the ongoing economic crisis, resident Mayas struggle against the Mexican state — rather than against tourists — that regularly "sweeps" them from the tourist zone in order to anchor the nation in an image of pure antiquity. This video also asks what kind of fieldwork is possible at such a spectacle, and it questions the status of ethnographic authority as people from the various groups converging on the event, including the anthropologist-videomakers, ironically trade positions as well as compete to speak about the Maya.

REASONS FOR ITS USEFULNESS:

Himpele and Castaneda's film is of particular value for anthropologists in that it takes as its subject something that is infrequently addressed by ethno-graphic filmmakers: the act of reconstructing the past and inscribing the present with it. Moreover, *Incidents of Travel at Chichen Itza* focuses NOT on the heirs of a specific cultural tradition, but upon outsiders who have chosen to embrace a tradition other than their own in order to satisfy an agenda of their own making. Himpele and Castaneda seize upon the irony of this situation wherein "outsiders" instruct "insiders" in the latter's own history, thereby testifying to the former's greater access to formal education and elite scholarly discourses. Consequently, the film raises questions regarding cultural authenticity, patrimony, and the significance of memory and lived experience for the creation of cultural and personal identities. Also of relevance to anthropology is the film's portrayal of an instance wherein the "traditional" roles of "us" and "other" are reversed as Westerners in search of cultural insight and difference become the agents of spectacle rather than its audience. In a similar vein, the film depicts a different role for anthropologists, as Himpele and Castaneda focus their attention, not on local area residents but, on the interlopers present at Chichen Itza who include New Age spiritualists as well as the filmmakers, themselves. Related to this is another anthropologically relevant feature — the film's focus upon the interaction between the local and the global. As incidents explicitly show, this particular constellation of external forces and internal exigencies has resulted in the following

46

phenomena: the spread of capitalism; resistance to the intrusion of the Mexican state; and the creation of new cultural forms.

QUESTIONS BEFORE SCREENING:

1. What is a pilgrimage? Who performs them, and why?
2. What is religious syncretism?
3. What is millenarism?
4. Describe the relationship between the sacred and the secular.
5. Discuss the term "cultural authenticity." Is it an ideal, or can it be realized? Who decides?

QUESTIONS AFTER SCREENING:

1. What is the significance of history for the nation-state?
2. How has Chichen Itza been transformed by archaeologists, state agencies, and tourists?
3. How can one identify with a people or a culture about which one has no experiential knowledge?
4. How do the rules and regulations governing the use of space at Chichen Itza reflect social and economic policies of the state? How do the tourists and local Mayas respond to these rules and regulations?
5. Why did the 1993 summer equinox appear as a sign of cultural renewal to tourists and local Maya alike?

Awards and Screenings: Society for Visual Anthropology Film Festival, Award, 1997
Margaret Mead Film Festival, 1997

Distributor: Documentary Educational Resources
　　　　　　Contact: Cynthia Close
*Note*: See distributor information at the end of the book.

* * * * * * * * * *

# JAGUAR

Jean Rouch, filmmaker
Distributor: Documentary Educational Resources
Format: 16mm film, video, color, 91 minutes, 1967
Genre: classic ethnographic film
Key Words: West Africa, Niger, Ghana, Migration, Wage Labor

SUMMARY:

Three young men from the Savannah of Niger leave their homeland to seek wealth and adventure on the coast and in the cities of Ghana. This film is the story of their travels, their encounters along the way, their experiences in Accra and Kumasi, and, after three months, their return to their families and friends at home. The film is part documentary, part fiction, and part reflective commentary. There was no portable sound synchronized equipment in the early 1950s when *Jaguar* was shot. Instead, Rouch had the main characters (his friends and "accomplices") improvise a narrative while they viewed the film, which was itself improvised along the way. The resulting soundtrack consists of remembered dialogue, of joking and exclamations, of questions and explanations about the action on the screen.

Short-term, rural migration to the cities is common to much of contemporary Africa. Here we meet Lam, the herdsman; Illo, the fisherman; and Damoure, their unsettled but literate friend. The three trek, for more than a month, south through Dahomey to Ghana, crossing the land of the Somba people (whose nudity shocks them), eating coconuts "more delicious than cheese," and delighting in the ocean with its waves and starfish. Eventually they part ways. Damoure and Illo go to Accra and Lam to Kumasi, where they find jobs as dockworker, foreman for a lumberman, and cattle herder for a city butcher. Having made their separate journey, they meet again in Kumasi, with a fourth friend, and set up an open-air stall, Petit a Petit, in which they hawk everything from alarm clocks to pictures of Queen Elizabeth.

Financially successful but homesick, the friends decide to leave the excitement, turmoil, and bewildering complexity of the city to return home to Niger before the rains. Lam rejoins his herd, enriched with a new umbrella and a lance; Illo, "magician of the river," catches a hippo and distributes everything he has brought from his journey to his family; and Damoure admires anew the beauty of Niger women. Yet although life in the village resumes as usual, Illo, Lam, and Damoure have been "jaguars" in the city: sophisticated "keen young men" with fancy hairdos, cigarettes, sunglasses, money, and knowledge of the urban world.

REASONS FOR ITS USEFULNESS:

The film raises, but does not answer, questions about the meaning of this experience and the transformations it may entail in the lives of the returned youths. *Jaguar*, Thomas Beidelman has written, "does succeed in catching the flavor of what it must be like to pass to and from a modern city and a rural village in Africa...*Jaguar* could be an eloquent document on the process of social change."

The flavor, it might be added, is very gay. Rouch has pointed out that *Jaguar* does not attempt to reveal the misery and pain of the annual migration or the boredom of village life in the dry season (eight months of the year) when young men, no longer warriors as in the past, have nothing to do. Few men, in actuality, become "jaguars" in the carefree style of Damoure, Lam, and Illo. For most, the city is a struggle. Yet *Jaguar* is nonetheless a vivid portrayal of the ideal of migration, a fantasy imparted through the improvised actions and spirited commentary of the characters. In this film Rouch has developed a form one might call "ethnographic fantasy," with an authenticity and reality as important as, although quite different from, that of Rouch's own monograph on rural migration to Accra.

QUESTIONS BEFORE SCREENING:

1. What are some of the possible functions of short-term migration for a culture?
2. How has the industrial mode of production changed migration patterns?

QUESTIONS AFTER SCREENING:

1.  What do we learn about cultural variation in Africa from the film?
2.  How is this film unique in its documentation and presentation of events?

FILMS RELATED BY GEOGRAPHIC OR SUBJECT AREA:

The Lion Hunters; LaPyramide Humaine; Petit a Petit: Madame L'Eau, all by Jean Rouch

Associated Reading: The Cinematic Griot: the Ethnography of Jean Rouch, by Paul Stoller, Chicago: The University of Chicago Press, 1992.

Distributor: Documentary Educational Resources
*Note*: See distributor information at the end of the book.

\* \* \* \* \* \* \* \* \* \* \*

## - 24 -

## JOE LEAHY'S NEIGHBORS

Bob Connolly and Robin Anderson, filmmakers
Distributor: Documentary Educational Resources
Format: video, color, 90 minutes, 1988
Genre: classic ethnographic film
Key Words: Papua New Guinea, Irian Jaya

SUMMARY:

Joe Leahy is the mixed race son of Australian miner Michael Leahy and a young highland girl. Joe, now in his fifties, is a wealthy coffee plantation owner. He lives in Western-style grandeur amidst his poorer Ganiga neighbors. Joe Leahy's links to his neighbors and their financial and emotional bonds are explored in this film by Connolly and Anderson, a follow-up to *First Contact*. The filmmakers lived in the highlands and filmed for eighteen months. They built a grass and thatch house on the edge of Joe Leahy's plantation — in the "no man's land" between Joe and the Ganiga. The film poignantly portrays both perspectives without value judgments or resolution for either side.

## REASONS FOR ITS USEFULNESS:

As a follow-up to *First Contact*, this film portrays some of the after effects of cultural contact. Social division based on wealth and racial difference is explored through the following of Joe Leahy as he interacts with his neighbors. Issues of economic exploitation and cultural change are foregrounded. This film is most fruitfully shown in conjunction with Connolly and Anderson's other films on the area, *First Contact* and *Black Harvest*.

## QUESTIONS BEFORE SCREENING:

1.  What are some of the main issues of cultural change facing indigenous groups in Papua New Guinea?
2.  How do people of mixed parentage fit into culture?

## QUESTIONS AFTER SCREENING:

1.  What do we learn about cultural survival from the film?
2.  What are some of the ethical issues of a film like this?

## FILMS RELATED BY GEOGRAPHIC OR SUBJECT AREA:

Dead Birds; Tidkawa and Friends; First Contact; Black Harvest

Distributor: Documentary Educational Resources
*Note*: See distributor information at the end of the book.

* * * * * * * * * * *

# LATCHO DRUMM
## LATCHO DROM (The Good Road)

Tony Gatlif, director
Distributor: Compagnie France Film
Format: video (sale only), color, 103 minutes, 1994
Genre: narrative, feature length documentary
Key Words: Asia, Egypt, Europe, Music, Roma (Gypsies)

SUMMARY:

Since they left northwestern India over a thousand years ago for unknown reasons, Roma (Gypsies) have traversed the roads of Asia, Europe, and Northern Africa. *Latcho Drom* retraces this long journey by focusing on Romani musical traditions spanning three continents, from northwest India to Spain. The film travels across eight countries and encounters the extraordinary variety of songs, dances, and music produced by Roma, a people whose history has gone unrepresented in books and written music alike. It is through their music and oral tradition that their history and experiences of persecution and suffering are preserved.

REASONS FOR ITS USEFULNESS:

*Latcho Drom* is a beautifully photographed and recorded film that is significant to anthropology because it concerns a diverse group of people who are so rarely sensitively and positively portrayed in the medium of film — the Roma (Gypsies). Made by a Romani filmmaker residing in Canada, this film is intended as a celebration of the rich musical traditions of Roma living throughout eight countries on three contiguous continents. Unlike many films that rely heavily upon dialogue and narration, *Latcho Drom* communicates solely through its visuals, music, and poignant lyrics which express not only the aspirations and values of specific Romani groups, but the pain of rejection and persecution encountered by Roma in most of the places where they have settled. While the film is not a conventional ethnographic film in that its goal is not exposition, it is instructive in its treatment of ethnicity and culture as mutable and

52

heterogeneous, rather than rigid and uniform, identities. As the film moves from one country to the next, it becomes clear that Roma share with each other as many commonalities (love of music, common Indic origin, history of marginalization) as differences (language, religion, residential patterns, style of music). Furthermore, the film confounds many of the stereotypes commonly held by Gadzhe (non-Roma) about Roma. For example, the film reveals that most Roma are sedentarized and live in cities as well as rural areas. It also reveals that, while they maintain a cultural distinctness, they have adopted many of the Gadzhe's conveniences and technologies, in some cases adopting them in order to continue their own "traditional" practices (e.g., replacing the horse and buggy with RVs for religious pilgrimages and rendezvous with far-flung friends and family). Furthermore, it underscores the fact that Roma are an ethnic group bound together through kinship, common beliefs and practices, and a history of Gadzhe persecution.

QUESTIONS BEFORE SCREENING:

1. What is peripatetic nomadism? How does it differ from pastoral nomadism?
2. From where did the term "Gypsy" originate? Why?
3. What is the difference between an ethnic group and a social group? Why is this distinction important when discussing Romani culture?
4. What kind of information may be revealed about a people through the study of their language?
5. What is a diaspora of people? How does it come about? What are some of the issues faced by people living in diaspora?

QUESTIONS AFTER SCREENING:

1. What kind of cultural differences do you notice as the film moves from one country to another? Think about employment, music, place of residence, etc.
2. What kinds of interactions does the film record between Roma and non-Roma?
3. Give examples of discrimination encountered by Roma in the film.
4. Who are the musicians in the film? How did they learn their skills?
5. Contrast what you saw in the film with what you previously thought about Roma (Gypsies).

FILMS RELATED BY GEOGRAPHIC OR SUBJECT AREA:

Across the Tracks: Vlach Gypsies in Hungary, by Michael Stewart, distributed by Films Incorporated
TÆan Bakhtale, by Alaina Lemon, distributed by Documentary Educational Resources

Distributor: Compagnie France Film
*Note*: See distributor information at the end of the book.

\* \* \* \* \* \* \* \* \* \*

---

## - 26 -

## LEAVING BAKUL BAGAN

Sandeep Ray, director
Distributor: Documentary Educational Resources
Format: video only (rental or sale), color, 43 minutes, 1994
Genre: contemporary, autobiographical, cinema verite
Key Words: India, Transculturalism, Communalism

SUMMARY:

Three generations of the extended Roychowdury family have resided for decades at 160 Bakul Bagan Road, Calcutta. Every now and then one of its members has to leave the landscape of their childhood — a large sprawling house built around a courtyard — and all the affection that dozens of relatives surround them with in order to relocate for a job or to start a family elsewhere. In *Leaving Bakul Bagan*, Saborna, a twenty-one year old girl, prepares to leave for higher studies in the United States. The film is an intimate portrayal of her interactions with her family during her last few days at home. It is full of casual conversational humor and vignettes from typical familial interactions. Incidental to the time and woven into the film are the effects of race riots throughout India in the aftermath of destruction of a Mosque by Hindu fanatics. This incident precipitates an already brewing political debate about the ethics of leaving for America, especially on the eve of such a tragic political disaster. The very last scene, rendered in slow motion to heighten its sensibility, effectively creates a sense of deep loss and the feeling that the need for familial roots are indeed pan-ethnic and trans-cultural. Even though shot in cinema-verite style, *Leaving Bakul Bagan* has the grace and the flow of a dramatic narrative.

REASONS FOR ITS USEFULNESS:

*Leaving Bakul Bagan* is an important ethnographic document in that it privileges a subjectivity that does not often figure prominently in ethnographic films; namely, that of a young unmarried woman. As the film's protagonist, Saborna introduces the audience to her world from her point of view, and Ray's observational shooting style combines with Saborna's charisma and enthusiasm over her impending departure to make the audience feel as if it were actually part of Saborna's milieu. This sensation is further heightened by the fact that the director does not attempt to narrate or contextualize the filmed events. Ray provides "clues" within the film, but the audience is expected to interpret them without the assistance or interference of the filmmaker. For example, Saborna never explicitly talks about her impressions of the United States; however, some of her expectations about living in the United States are revealed when the camera records her making some last minute preparations for her trip. Yet, the film does not end as it began, for it shifts dramatically in intensity and rhetorical style during the confrontation between Saborna and her brother. With its charged dialogue concerning the future of India and the harmful effects of capitalism, this scene provides *Leaving Bakul Bagan* with its intellectual grist and makes it of university relevance to cultural studies.

QUESTIONS BEFORE SCREENING:

1. What is communal violence? Under what circumstances is it likely to occur?
2. What does it mean to "westernize" or be "westernized?"
3. Discuss the following economic terms: third world country; lesser developed country; under developed country; and developing country. To what do these terms refer, and what do they describe? What stereotypes do they rely on or give rise to?
4. What does it mean for a people to live in diaspora? Give several

reasons why a people might have chosen/been forced to exist in this condition.

5. What kind of family structures or family arrangements are most prevalent in the United States? What relationships do these types of families bear to the economy and political system?

QUESTIONS AFTER SCREENING:

1. Describe the type of building the Roychowdhury family lives in. Who lives there, and how do they interact with each other?
2. Based on the film, name several examples of lasting British influence on contemporary Indian culture.
3. What is meant by the expression "brain drain," and what effect does it have upon the two countries involved?
4. Summarize the argument between Saborna and her brother over her choice to study in the United States, and do not forget to discuss the conflict between individual and national interests.
5. What do you believe the relationship between history and the present to be?

FILMS RELATED BY GEOGRAPHIC OR SUBJECT AREA:

Video SEWA, by Self Employed Women's Association
Photo Wallahs, by David and Judith MacDougall
Kamala and Raji, by Michael Camarini and Shari Robertson

Awards: Best of Category, New England Film and Video Festival, 1994
Special Invitation, 40th Flaherty Film Seminar, 1994
RAI, University of Kent Festival of Ethnographic Films, 1994
Whitney Museum Tour, New York, Bombay, New Delhi, 1994

Distributor: Documentary Educational Resources
       Contact: Cynthia Close
*Note*: See distributor information at the end of the book.

\* \* \* \* \* \* \* \* \* \* \*

# 27

# LES MAITRES FOUS (THE MAD MASTERS)

Jean Rouch, filmmaker
Distributor: Documentary Educational Resources
Format: 16mm film, video, color, 35 minutes, 1957
Genre: classic ethnographic film
Key Words: West Africa, Ghana, Possession, Trance, Colonialism

SUMMARY:

*Les Maitres Fous* is about the ceremony of a religious sect, the Hauka, which was widespread in West Africa from the 1920s to the 1950s. Hauka participants were usually rural migrants from Niger who came to the cities, such as Accra in Ghana (then Gold Coast), where they found work as laborers in the city's lumber yards, as stevedores at the docks, or in the mines. There were at least 30,000 practicing Hauka in Accra in 1954 when Jean Rouch was asked by a small group to film their annual ceremony. During this ritual, which took place on a farm a few hours from the city, the Hauka entered trance and were possessed by various spirits associated with the Western colonial powers: the governor-general, the engineer, the doctor's wife, the wicked major, the corporal of the guard.

The roots of the Hauka lie in traditional possession cults common among the Songhay and Djerma peoples of the Niger River basin. Gifted men and women may enter trance and become possessed by any of a number of strong gods, such as Dongo, god of thunder and the sky. Supplicants consult the god through the trancing medium and receive advice about their problems, cures for diseases, comfort and support, or reprimands for their wrong doings. Like these traditional possession cults, the Hauka sect coexisted with Islam and incorporated many Islamic saints and heroes into its rituals. Most of its adherents were Muslims.

REASONS FOR ITS USEFULNESS:

The imagery in *Les Maitres Fous* is powerful and often disturbing:

57

possessed men with rolling eyes and foaming at the mouth, eating a sacrificed dog (in violation of taboo), burning their bodies with flaming torches. Beyond the imagery, the themes are also powerful and have had an impact in our own culture: Jean Genet's *The Blacks* was modeled upon the Hauka inversion in which blacks assume the role of masters, and Peter Brook's *Marat/Sade* was influenced by the theatricality and invented language of Hauka possession. Yet, as Rouch reminds us in an interview in Cineaste, possession for the Hauka cultists was not theater but reality. The significance of this reality is left ambiguous in the film, although Rouch's commentary suggests that the ritual provides a psychological release which enables the Hauka to be good workers and to endure a degrading situation with dignity. The unexplored relation of the Hauka movement to their colonial experience is perhaps the most intriguing issue raised by this ceremony in which the oppressed become, for a day, the possessed and the powerful.

QUESTIONS BEFORE SCREENING:

1. What is trance?
2. What is spirit possession?

QUESTIONS AFTER SCREENING:

1. What do we learn about trance and spirit possession from this film?
2. What do we learn about colonialism from this film?

FILMS RELATED BY GEOGRAPHIC OR SUBJECT AREA:

The Lion Hunters; Jaguar; Petit a Petit; The Human Pyramid; Madame L'Eau, all by Jean Rouch

Associated Reading: The Cinematic Griot: the Ethnography of Jean Rouch, by Paul Stoller, Chicago: The University of Chicago Press, 1992.

Distributor: Documentary Educational Resources
*Note*: See distributor information at the end of the book.

\* \* \* \* \* \* \* \* \* \*

# 28

## LIGHTING THE SEVENTH FIRE

Sandra Osawa, director
Distributor: Upstream Productions
Format: video, color, 47:30 minutes, 1994
Genre: contemporary, indigenous
Key Words:      Fishing Rights, Law - U.S. Treaty Law, Native
                 Americans - Chippewa, Racism, United States - Great
                 Lakes

SUMMARY:

A Chippewa prophecy foretells a time called the Seventh Fire, when lost traditions will be recovered. Native American filmmaker, Sandra Osawa, examines how the Chippewa Indians of Northern Wisconsin have struggled to restore the centuries old tradition of spearfishing and the heated opposition they have encountered.

REASONS FOR ITS USEFULNESS:

*Lighting the Seventh Fire* is an interesting and instructive film for a number of reasons. First, unlike many classic ethnographic films which aspire to paint a neutral and descriptive portrait of a given society, *Lighting the Seventh Fire* focuses upon an issue of great political and cultural relevance to the subjects of the film, thereby making a positive contribution to their, rather than simply "our," community. Second, it shows how Native Americans have appealed to the United States legal system in their efforts to have their rights respected. Moreover, it shows how, in the face of conflicting jurisdictional claims, the Chippewa have turned to the federal court system for its ability to overrule Wisconsin's violation of treaties signed between the Chippewa nation and the U.S. federal government. Third, *Lighting the Seventh Fire* reveals the injustice and irony in people's condemnation of Chippewa spearfishers for the depletion of the Great Lakes' walleyes when sportfishing and fishing industries proliferate in the area and, thus, provides the basis for a class discussion on how a troubled economy can create an environment in which racial/ethnic tensions are transformed into hostile confrontations between members of different communities. Fourth, Osawa's film is a poignant testament to our country's continuing inability to recognize and accommodate cultural differences.

QUESTIONS BEFORE SCREENING:

1. What are the distinctions between the following terms: nation, state, and nation-state? Give examples of each.
2. What is a mode of production? Name several and discuss their characteristics.
3. What is the legal status of Native American reservations?
4. What is a treaty? Who has the power to make them, and who is charged with their enforcement?
5. What is a prophecy?

QUESTIONS AFTER SCREENING:

1. Discuss the legal jurisdiction of the state and the federal government with respect to the Chippewa reservation and ceded lands in Wisconsin.
2. How has spearfishing been adapted to the needs of contemporary Chippewas?
3. Discuss the function of the drums during confrontations the Chippewa have with nonIndians at the boat landings.
4. Why do some of the protesters of spearfishing believe that Chippewas have received preferential treatment by the Chicago Circuit Court's ruling in favor of Chippewa hunting and fishing rights in the ceded territories?
5. What roles do tourism and the fishing industry play in Wisconsin — particularly in northern Wisconsin along the lake shores?

FILMS RELATED BY GEOGRAPHIC OR SUBJECT AREA:

The Peyote Road, by Fidel Moreno
Imagining Indians, by Victor Masayesva

Awards: Nationally Broadcast on PBS Stations as part of the award-winning Point of View Series

Award of Excellence, National Indian Education Association
Runner-Up, Best Short Documentary, Red Earth Film and Video

Distributor: Upstream Productions
Note: See distributor information at the end of the book.

\* \* \* \* \* \* \* \* \* \* \*

# 29

## LORANG'S WAY

David and Judith MacDougall, filmmakers
Distributor: UCEMC
Format: 16mm, 1/2 inch VHS, color, 66 minutes, 1977
Genre: classic anthropological film
Key Words: Pastoralism, Age Grades, Tribe, Nation, State

SUMMARY:

A portrait of Lorang, the head of a homestead and a member of the
Turkana tribe, seminomadic herders of northwestern Kenya. Having
confronted the outside world, Lorang sees his traditional society as
vulnerable to change in the future. The film explores Lorang's personality
and ideas through conversations with the filmmakers, testimony of his
friends and relatives, and observation of his behavior with his wives, his
children, and men of his own age and status.

REASONS FOR ITS USEFULNESS:

Through the person of Lorang, this film documents the life of the Turkana
and thus is useful as an "experience" of pastoralism. It can be used to
discuss a range of related topics including: the human domestication of
generally slow-moving herbivores; the workings of an economy based on
animals; ecological balance between humans, their animals, and the land;
and social structure and kin relations in semi-nomadic societies. In the
film we come to know Lorang through other men of his age grade and
below, his wives and their households, and men from other Turkana

settlements. This provides a wealth of information with which to explore polygamy; kinship roles and expectations; and the matrix of political, social, and economic functions located in kinship in such a pastoral society.

Additionally, the film explores Lorang's reintegration into Turkana society after he is drafted into Kenya's military; discussions with younger men about changing "traditions" and their interactions with Kenyans and cities; and participation in an intra settlement political meeting where the discussion concerns raids against other "tribes" and particularly corrupt Turkana who have been recruited by the State as tax collectors. Thus, the film can be used to explore relationships between settlements and "tribes," as well as between peoples such as the Turkana and the Nation-State of Kenya. Both the persistence and the "invention" of tradition are illustrated here.

The film itself is structured so as to reveal its structure with intertitles serving as an outline of its organization and subtitled interviews serving as the primary source of information. Lorang, with his rags to riches story, serves as a subjective center helping to draw the audience into the film, personalizing a foreign culture. The constricted representation of Turkana society as one individual is problematic and should be discussed. However, it can provide a basis for a discussion of anthropological methodology and the various ways in which the limitations of totalizing narratives can be pushed back. For instance, by focusing on the variety of individuals who provide us information about Lorang, their various positions and points of view, the audience can begin to reflect upon the notion of The Turkana.

QUESTIONS BEFORE SCREENING:

1. How do we subsist? From whom do we obtain our necessities? What kinds of relationships do we have with them?
2. Who makes up a family? What are their responsibilities to each other?
3. How does the state regulate our behavior? How do relationships between the State and ethnic or other groups — Amish, militias — play out?
4. What is taxation for and what does it provide?
5. How do people end up in the military?

QUESTIONS AFTER SCREENING:

1. Discuss the topics of social change, modernization, and the place of the Turkana and their integration into global economy in order to deconstruct "folk knowledge" about unchanging tradition, progress, and wisdom.
2. How does the filmic or iconic representation in the film stimulate discussion on a variety of topics, such as mediation, written versus filmic narrative, representation, and so on?

FILMS RELATED BY GEOGRAPHIC OR SUBJECT AREA:

This film is the first in a trilogy titled Turkana Conversations by David and Judith MacDougall. Other films which deal with contact and social change include: N!ai and Pull Ourselves Up or Die by John Marshal; Cannibal Tours by Dennis O'Rourke; Jaguar by John Rouch; First Contact. Films which focus on modes of subsistence include: Hunters, Meat Fight and Bitter Melons by John Marshal; Nanook of the North by John Flarity; The Netsilik Eskimo Series; and The Plow that Broke the Plains.

Distributor: University of California Extention Media Center
Note: See distributor information at the end of the book.

\* \* \* \* \* \* \* \* \* \*

___

## - 30 -

## MADAME L'EAU (MADAME WIND)

Jean Rouch, filmmaker
Distributor: contact Documentary Educational Resources for latest information
Format: 16mm film, video, color, 100 minutes, 1993
Genre: classic ethnographic film
Key Words: West Africa, Niger, Holland, Draught, Development

SUMMARY:

Three of Jean Rouch's long time collaborators are facing a prolonged draught as the upper Niger River is reduced to a trickle. Crops are failing. Something must be done. The protagonists decide to travel to Holland to seek support in building low tech windmills to pump water from the river to nearby fields. The film follows them as they visit an overseas development agency and ask for support. They find someone to help design and build the windmill out of available materials. After returning to Niger, the windmill is built. One of the characters does some divining to determine the fate of the project. The project proves to be successful; but is it enough? The first crop is of black tulips, a gift from Holland.

REASONS FOR ITS USEFULNESS:

Sustainable and appropriate development has been quite elusive for many Third World countries. Often, like in Nigeria, development projects are massive in scale, are environmentally harmful, and are of little benefit to those on the lower end of the economic scale. In this film, Jean Rouch implicitly critiques massive development projects by participating in a development project on a small scale. He, and the other protagonists in the film also challenge prevailing ideologies of progress and technological innovation. An intermediate technology, inexpensive but effective, can make the difference for a poor farmer. The film teaches us this lesson through example.

QUESTIONS BEFORE SCREENING:

1.  How can industrialized communities contribute to the well-being of nonindustrialized communities?
2.  How does our government approach economic assistance to Third World countries?

QUESTIONS AFTER SCREENING:

1.  What is fact, and what is fiction in this film?
2.  What do we learn about economic cooperation from this film?

FILMS RELATED BY GEOGRAPHIC OR SUBJECT AREA:

The Lion Hunters; Jaguar; Petit a Petit; The Human Pyramid; Les Maitres Fous, all by Jean Rouch

Associated Reading: The Cinematic Griot: the Ethnography of Jean Rouch, by Paul Stoller, Chicago: The University of Chicago Press, 1992.

Distributor: Documentary Educational Resources
Note: See distributor information at the end of the book.

* * * * * * * * * * *

- 31 -

## MAGICAL DEATH

Tim Asch, filmmaker; Napoleon Chagnon, anthropologist
Distributor: Documentary Educational Resources
Format: 16mm, 1/2 VHS, 3/4 U-matic, color, 28 minutes, 1973
Genre: classic
Key Words: Hallucinogens, Ritual, Shamanism, Trance, Ritual Warfare

SUMMARY:

Focuses on the role of an older Yanomamo Indian, Dedeheiwa, who is a prominent political leader and renowned shaman from a village in the Orinoco River area of southern Venezuela and northeastern Brazil. Documents the activities that take place in a two-day period during which Dedeheiwa organizes many of the co-villagers in a joint magical attack on the souls of children in a distant village. Shows use of hallucinogenic snuff by shamans. Suited for courses relating religious activities to political and social organization. From the Yanomamo series.

REASONS FOR ITS USEFULNESS:

This film is largely observational with sparse voice over narration and a few subtitled comments. As it covers difficult terrain and the filmmakers seem to have difficulty contextualizing the material so as not to alienate and increase ethnocentric stereotypes, this film is not entirely appropriate for introductory level courses. Nevertheless, it is an important visual document once viewers have developed critical viewing skills and are familiar with more recent anthropological insights. Substances which alter consciousness, a few of which are currently the subject of a rather confusing debate in the U.S., are an integral and important part of Yanomamo society. Though the film shows only the external, "real," objective events involved as a shaman exerts his combined political, curing, debilitating, and magical powers, viewers with some background will sense the power of the events taking place. Observations can be made about the social roles of shamans both within their own groups as well as their roles in relations to other groups; comparisons of ritual protocol, trance activities and behavior, magical warfare juxtaposed to actual warfare, and sanctions and controls applied to altered states can be made with other films of this sort of activity.

QUESTIONS BEFORE SCREENING:

1. What are ways in which people alter their consciousness? Is this an old human practice? Why do people do it?
2. What are people referring to in the U.S. when they talk about drugs? Does this include all mind altering substances? What are acceptable ways of altering your consciousness in our society?
3. What is a shaman? What social roles do they play?
4. What is a ritual? Are there common features? What do rituals provide their participants?
5. What is "black magic" or voodoo? Is there a stereotype, and what is the real practice like?

QUESTIONS AFTER SCREENING:

1. Do you think the film accurately documents all the events taking place? What is missing?
2. What are Dedeheiwa's roles in Yanomamo society? Is there any comparable role in our society?
3. Are the events you witnessed spiritual in nature? How does their combination of magical/actual warfare compare with ours (prayers for victory and safety, army chaplains)?

4. Do there appear to be noticeable procedures? Are there stages or discernible periods of events which might be common to larger patterns of rituals?
5. Do the ritual proceedings benefit the participants and their respective groups? How?

Distributor: Documentary Educational Resources
*Note*: See distributor information at the end of the book.

\* \* \* \* \* \* \* \* \* \* \*

---

## - 32 -

## MORNING WITH ASCH
---

Jayasinhji Jhala and Lindsey Powell, producer/directors
Distributor: Documentary Educational Resources
Format: 1/2 VHS, color, 45 minutes, 1995
Genre: films about anthropological filmmakers
Key Words:   Ethnographic Film, Representation, Dying, Swan Song, Collaboration, Context

SUMMARY:

In the Spring of 1994, Timothy Asch, internationally known and honored filmmaker, co-founder of Documentary Educational Resources, educator, anthropologist, and driving force behind the Visual Anthropology Review, was dying of cancer. His colleague and fellow visual anthropologist, Jayasinhji Jhala visited him at his home in Los Angeles to conduct a videotaped interview from which this edited version is the end result. Tim took this opportunity to express his views about his life and work, revealing intimate details that give us a perspective not only on this complex individual but on the reality of confronting death. Jhala, professor of anthropology at Temple University, makes us very much aware of the influence of the filmmaker on the filmed subject and vice versa. Collaboration was a central theme for Tim Asch, beginning with anthropologist Napoleon Chagnon and their ground breaking fieldwork with the Yanomamo. The resulting films from the 1970s are still widely used. Later, he worked in Indonesia with Linda Connor, his wife Patsy Asch, and E. Douglas Lewis. Excerpts from Asch's films, representing each of these periods, are woven into the dialogue. See also Visual Anthropology Review, vol. 11, number 1, spring 1995.

## REASONS FOR ITS USEFULNESS:

*Morning with Asch* is a film for those advanced in their consideration of issues of representation particularly in regard to filmic ethnography. The film is powerful for the simplicity, honesty, and intimacy established with a man passing from a life which has been so central to the development of aural/pictoial portraits of culture. Reviewing his efforts in the field, working with several different anthropologists, Asch identifies specific problems with his pioneering efforts with Napoleon Chagnon. While he acknowledges problems in the films, such as the fierceness stereotype, he also points out early attempts to personalize people — for instance through humor — whose lifeways are so very different from our own. Through his work with anthropologists of different genders, the film also addresses the effects of socialization processes prior to disciplinary training. This is highlighted by Tim's reevaluation of a considerable number of details and significant events of his own early life circumstances. Some might evaluate the film as a morbid one as we have so shut the process of dying out of our own culture. Yet his near death confrontation with the camera, Asch's own look, is revelatory in assessing the efforts one might make with one's own life. Acknowledging that ethnographic filmmakers have yet to produce so holistic a statement of a culture as fiction producers such as Satyajit Ray, his final words are those of encouragement for those who make the attempt.

## QUESTIONS BEFORE SCREENING:

1. How might different formats — books, photographs, films — for ethnographic expression effect the perception of the subjects?
2. How can an ethnographer's own cultural and personal circumstances effect their interpretation of a different culture?
3. What are positive and negative aspects of collaboration between filmmakers and anthropologists?
4. What commonalities do the films of Timothy Asch share? How do they change over the course of his career?

5. What is the place of representation in the process of dying?

QUESTIONS AFTER SCREENING:

1. What are ways in which Asch indicates future visual anthropologists might strive to create empathetic connections and holistic understanding across cultures?
2. How does Tim's condition effect you as a viewer? Does this film break conventions, which and how?
3. How do you think Tim Asch's own background has influenced his filmmaking?
4. Have you noticed differences in anthropological filmmaking attributable to the class, race, gender, or other personal circumstances of the maker? Are these factors typically known by the viewer?
5. Should there by more of a relationship between fiction and ethnographic filmmaking? How could it develop? What are the limits?

Distributor: Documentary Educational Resources
*Note*: See distributor information at the end of the book.

\* \* \* \* \* \* \* \* \* \*

---

- 33 -

## MYSTIC VISION, SACRED ART

Raju Gurung and Anne Kaufman
Distributor: Documentary Educational Resources
Format: video only (rental or sale), color, 28 minutes, 1996
Genre: contemporary
Key Words:      Art - Sacred, Tibetan Buddhism, Nepal, South Asia, Thangka Paintings

SUMMARY:

This documentary provides an excellent introduction to the art of thangka, sacred Tibetan Buddhist painting in the Kathmandu Valley of Nepal. Carefully filmed, it takes you through every step of the painting process of thangkas. It offers insight into the symbolic and religious meaning of thangkas and their importance for Tibetan Buddhist life. Most of the artists in this documentary are Tibetan refugees who have devoted their lives to preserving this sacred tradition. Thangkas are the scrolled devotional paintings used in Tibetan Buddhist ritual practice. Their bright colors and flowing patterns may be familiar and appreciated by westerners. However, the opportunity to see where, how, and by whom they are made effects our perception and understanding of the place these works hold in the practice of Buddhism. This documentary provides detailed descriptions of technique from the stretching and preparation of the painting surface, to the grinding of the pigments, to the drawing of the image, and to its realization in brilliant colors.

REASONS FOR ITS USEFULNESS:

*Mystic Vision, Sacred Art* is of interest to anthropologists because it explores the relationship between art and religion through its discussion of the ways in which thangka paintings assist Tibetan Buddhists in attaining their religious objectives, such as: teaching the history of Tibetan Buddhism and its religious principles; attaining religious merit; bringing visions seen by mystics and saints within reach of all Tibetan Buddhists; and, aiding in prayer by reminding the person of all the qualities that help overcome worldly attachment and suffering. The film also draws the audience's attention to the distinction between secular and sacred objects and shows how integral ritualized language and behavior is to the transformation of the former into the latter. Furthermore, *Mystic Vision* shows that thangka painting differs from modern painting traditions in that thangka painting is taught through an apprenticeship system (rather than classroom education), has a strict iconography, and is a group endeavor, entailing the collaboration of many on such painting. However, the film in no way suggests that such paintings are the product of rote imitation. On the contrary, it suggests that even though painters must conform to certain conventions, they are involved in a creative process that is as artistic as it is spiritual. Consequently, *Mystic Vision* leaves the viewer wondering whether thangka painting, or any other "sacred art," is really so qualitatively different from the Western "secular art" tradition.

QUESTIONS BEFORE SCREENING:

1. What are some of the most prominent features of Buddhism?
2. What is esoteric Knowledge with respect to religion?
3. What is iconography?
4. What is the goal of Buddhist meditation?
5. What is the Buddhist pantheon? What are divine incarnations?

QUESTIONS AFTER SCREENING:

1. Why is Nepal, particularly Kathmandu, an important center for Tibetan Buddhism? What event of major importance has transpired in Tibet between 1959 and the present?
2. Describe the Thangka painting apprenticeship system. How does such a system of instruction compare/contrast with classroom education?
3. What is the religious significance of thangka paintings?
4. What constitutes a "correct" thangka painting?
5. What must occur if the thangka painting is to be endowed with the spirit of the divinity it depicts?

FILMS RELATED BY GEOGRAPHIC OR SUBJECT AREA:

Requiem for a Faith, Distributor Hartley Productions
Sherpas, by Sherry Ortner, Distributor Films Incorporated

Distributor: Documentary Educational Resources
                    Contact: Cynthia Close
*Note*: See distributor information at the end of the book.

* * * * * * * * * *

# 34

# N!AI, THE STORY OF A !KUNG WOMAN

John Marshall, filmmaker
Distributor: Documentary Educational Resources
Format: 16mm film, video, color, 59 minutes, 1980
Genre: classic ethnographic film
Key Words:     Southern Africa, !Kung, Ju/Æhoansi, Hunting and
Gathering, Gender, Life History

## SUMMARY:

This film provides a broad overview of !Kung life, both past and present,
and an intimate portrait of N!ai, a !Kung woman who in 1978 was in her
mid-thirties. N!ai tells her own story and, in so doing, the story of changes
in !Kung life over a thirty year period. "Before the white people came, we
did what we wanted," N!ai recalls, describing the life she remembers as a
child: following her mother to pick berries, roots, and nuts as the season
changed; the division of giraffe meat; the kinds of rain; her resistance to
her marriage to /Gunda at the age of eight; and her changing feelings
about her husband when he becomes a healer. As N!ai speaks, the film
presents scenes from the 1950s that show her as a young girl and a young
wife. The uniqueness of N!ai may lie in its tight integration of
ethnography and history. While it portrays the changes in !Kung society
over thirty years, it never loses sight of the individual, N!ai.

## REASONS FOR ITS USEFULNESS:

Few ethnographic films have concentrated on an individual. This film is
unique in that it concentrates on a middle aged woman but, by so doing,
reveals a great deal about the culture of which she is a part. It is a frank
and honest portrait of N!ai by a man that knew her well. We learn from
her much about the ethnographic gaze as well, as she challenges the
camera (and by extension the viewer) not to look at her. She wants to tell
her story, yet is also resistant.

QUESTIONS BEFORE SCREENING:

1. What are some of the ways in which life history can reveal things about culture that a synchronic ethnography cannot?
2. How do the roles that an individual has in a community differ at the various stages of a life?

QUESTIONS AFTER SCREENING:

1. What are some of the ways in which traditional cultures have adapted to changing circumstances in their relationships with other cultures.
2. What does this film suggest to us about audience and the ethnographic gaze?

FILMS RELATED BY GEOGRAPHIC OR SUBJECT AREA:

The Hunters; The Meat Fight; A Joking Relationship; Bitter Melons; N/um. Tchai; An Argument about a Marriage; Pull Ourselves Up or Die Out, all by John Marshall.

Awards: Grand Prize, Cinema du Reel (Paris); Blue Ribbon, American Film Festival; CINE Golden Eagle Award; Gold Medal for Best Television Documentary, International Film and Television Festival of New York; Grand Prize, International News Coverage Festival (Luchon, France); Film Commendation from Royal Anthropological Institute (London)

Reviews: American Anthropologist, Volume 83, Number 3, Sept. 1981, pg. 740-741, by Robert Gordon; Journal of American Folklore, Volume 97, Number 383, 1984, pg. 106-108, by Keith Cummingham; Choice, July/Aug. 1982, pg. 44-47, by Paul Brubaker; Guide to N!ai, reviewed American Anthropologist, Volume 88, June 1986, pg. 516-517, by Megan Biesele.

Associated Reading: The Cinema of John Marshall, edited by Jay Ruby, Philadelphia: Harwood Academic Publishers, 1993; The Harmless People, Elizabeth Marshall Thomas, New York: Alfred A. Knopf, 1959.

Distributor: Documentary Educational Resources
*Note*: See distributor information at the end of the book.

\* \* \* \* \* \* \* \* \* \*

# 35

# NO LOANS TODAY: SOUTH CENTRAL LOS ANGELES

Lisanne Skyler, director
<u>Distributor</u>: First Run Features/Icarus Films
<u>Format</u>: video only (rental), color, 55 minutes, 1995
<u>Genre</u>: contemporary
<u>Key Words</u>:    African-Americans, Urban Areas, Economics,
                Entrepreneurship, Africana Studies

## SUMMARY:

Documents daily life in the African-American community of South
Central Los Angeles, focusing on the ABC Loan Company, a twenty-five-
year-old pawnshop and check cashing outlet. Explores the lives of people
who have either chosen or been forced to remain in the area and examines
the impact of such problems as crime and unemployment on businesses
like ABC. Presents the pawnshop as a metaphor for survival and reveals
an unseen resiliency in South Central's residents.

## REASONS FOR ITS USEFULNESS:

Prior to the riots which broke out in South Central Los Angeles in 1992,
many young Americans were unacquainted with this area of the country;
thereby ensuring that the media blitz following the riots provided its
audience with its first (and, possibly only) impression of South Central —
one which was overwhelmingly negative. Lisanne Skyler's film is
significant in that it helps to re-present South Central in a more
sympathetic and sincere manner. However, the film goes beyond being
just an effort to redeem the sullied reputation of an urban neighborhood.
For one, it testifies to the importance of viewing specific places and events
through the lens of history. Through interviews with local residents and
business owners, the audience becomes aware of the fact that South
Central has not always been an impoverished neighborhood. On the
contrary, as recently as the 1970s, it was an economically stable
community in which residents earned a living wage in several large local

companies and factories. Yet, when these companies and their jobs relocated, many of South Central's residents were unable to accompany them. By including this testimony in her film, Skyler links the fate of South Central to events transpiring on the national and global level and demonstrates that the world is far more interconnected than it is sometimes given credit for being. Additionally, the film addresses the very real negative impact of discrimination by raising the issue of redlining. As one man states, those wishing to do business in South Central are denied loans by lending institutions that judge South Central to be too "risky" for investment. Consequently, these would-be-entrepreneurs find it exceedingly difficult to raise the necessary start-up capital in order to open a business that would provide sorely needed jobs for South Central's residents. Finally, the film attests to the ingenuity of many of those living in South Central in their efforts to survive in an environment over which they have far from complete control.

QUESTIONS BEFORE SCREENING:

1. What is redlining?
2. What is residential segregation, and how does it reflect/support social, ethnic, and class hierarchies?
3. How is Los Angeles, as a city, represented in the media?
4. Name some examples of class discrimination — people unable to obtain a necessary service/employment due to their CLASS as opposed race/ethnicity.
5. What are some reasons for the existence of street gangs?

QUESTIONS AFTER SCREENING:

1. What role does ABC Loan Company fulfill in the community?
2. According to the film, what can happen in a woman's life to cause her to decide to stay on welfare?
3. Why were several of the people in the film unable to obtain loans from banks or other lending institutions?
4. Discuss the pressure placed on young black men to "provide" economically for their families.
5. Who do you think Lisanne Skyler is, and why or how do you think she made this film?

Distributor: First Run Features/Icarus Films
        Contact: Jennifer Houhlihan
*Note*: See distributor information at the end of the book.

\* \* \* \* \* \* \* \* \* \*

## - 36 -

## N/UM TCHAI: THE CEREMONIAL CURING DANCE
## OF THE !KUNG BUSHMEN

John Marshall, filmmaker
Distributor: Documentary Educational Resources
Format: 16mm film, video, black and white, 20 minutes, 1969
Genre: classic ethnographic film
Key Words:     Southern Africa, !Kung, Ju/Æhoansi, Hunting and
             Gathering, Music, Curing, Trance

SUMMARY:

Tchai is the word used by the !Kung to describe getting together to dance
and sing; n/um can be translated as medicine, or supernatural potency.
The !Kung gather for "medicine dances" often, usually at night, and
sometimes such dances last until dawn. Women sit on the ground,
clapping and singing and occasionally dancing a round or two, while men
circle around them, singing and stamping rhythms with their feet. The
songs are wordless but named: "rain," "sun," "honey," "giraffe," and
other "strong things." The strength of the songs is their n/um, or medicine,
thought to be a gift from the great god. N/um is also in the fire and, even
more so, in the "owners of medicine," or curers. Most !Kung men practice
as curers at some point in their lives, and in this film we see several men
in various stages of trance. A light trance gradually deepens, as the
medicine grows "hot," and eventually some men will shriek and run about,
falling on hot coals, entering the state the !Kung call "half-death."

The film opens with a brief introduction to the role of n/um tchai in
healing and in warding off evil, followed by scenes from one all-night

76

dance. The dance begins with a social gathering and becomes increasingly intense as the night wears on, finally concluding at dawn.

REASONS FOR ITS USEFULNESS:

Traditional medical practices are of great interest to anthropologists as well as to many others. Though the Ju/Æhoansi have developed a number of medicinal and other forms of physical treatments and also have had some access to treatments from other cultures, in this film we witness a type of curing that works on a spiritual or emotional level. The film is beautifully shot by a person that was very intimate with the people depicted, and it offers one a rare glimpse into this culture's healing time.

QUESTIONS BEFORE SCREENING:

1. In a culture where the division of labor is based on age, gender, and merit, what are some of the possible duties of a culturally competent young man?
2. What are some of the possible forms of medical intervention in a hunting and gathering culture with limited technology?

QUESTIONS AFTER SCREENING:

1. What is it about rhythm, music, and dance that could lead to healing powers?
2. What is the role of the individual in a group like the Ju/Æhoansi?

FILMS RELATED BY GEOGRAPHIC OR SUBJECT AREA:

The Hunters; The Meat Fight; A Joking Relationship; Bitter Melons; An Argument About a Marriage; N!ai, the Story of a !Kung Woman; Pull Ourselves Up or Die Out, all by John Marshall

Reviews: American Anthropologist, Volume 74, Numbers 1-2, September 1972, Pg. 193-194, by Livingston Film Collective, Rutgers University.
Associated Reading: The Cinema of John Marshall, edited by Jay Ruby, Philadelphia: Harwood Academic Publishers, 1993; The Harmless People, Elizabeth Marshall Thomas, New York: Alfred A. Knopf, 1959.

Distributor: Documentary Educational Resources
*Note*: See distributor information at the end of the book.

\* \* \* \* \* \* \* \* \* \* \*

---

## - 37 -

---

## NANOOK OF THE NORTH

---

Robert Flaherty, filmmaker
Distributor: Contact Documentary Educational Resources for latest
information
Format: video, color, 96 minutes, 1922
Genre: classic ethnographic film
Key Words: Canada, Eskimo, Inuit

SUMMARY:

This classic of the genre is one of the first attempts at cooperative or
participatory cinema. Flaherty spent several years living and traveling
with Nanook and his family as they hunted, fished, built igloos, and
survived in harsh arctic conditions. Flaherty screened his rushes with the
subjects and received their advice on how to shoot things better. The film
depicts many aspects of Native American life, primarily concentrating on
cooperative living.

REASONS FOR ITS USEFULNESS:

For those interested in traditional modes of subsistence like hunting and
gathering, this is the classic of the genre. Though involved in trade
relations with Canadians, the Inuit depicted are still practicing ancient
forms of subsistence. We see how salmon is fished for, how seals are
hunted, how dog sleds are packed and manipulated in the harshest of
conditions, how igloos are manufactured, etc. Courage and personal
strength guide Nanook and his family through extreme hardship.

QUESTIONS BEFORE SCREENING:

1. What is the hunting and gathering mode of subsistence?
2. How has the loss of traditional hunting and gathering territories affected aboriginal Americans?

QUESTIONS AFTER SCREENING:

1. What are some of the rewards of living in the arctic?
2. How does participatory cinema affect the authority of a film?

Distributor: Documentary Educational Resources
*Note*: See distributor information at the end of the book.

\* \* \* \* \* \* \* \* \* \*

---

## - 38 -

## NUMBER OUR DAYS

Barbara Myerhoff, anthropologist; Lynne Littman, filmmaker
Distributor: Direct Cinema Limited
Format: 16mm, 1/2 VHS, color, 29 minutes, 1977
Genre: ahead of its time/classic
Key Words: Diaspora, Ethnicity, Aging, Death, Tradition, Fieldwork

SUMMARY:

*Number Our Days* is a sensitive and compassionate portrait of a California community of elderly European Jews sustaining their vivid cultural heritage amid poverty and loneliness in modern America. The first collaboration between anthropologist Barbara Myerhoff and filmmaker Lynne Littman, this moving documentary illuminates the lives of these "indomitable survivors" with gentleness and honesty.

## REASONS FOR ITS USEFULNESS:

The specter of death looms about us all. Yet the fascination with death in the U.S. is when it is sudden, sexy, spectacular, and unexpected. It does not include "a series of losses" Barbara Myerhoff refers to as aging. By focusing upon a community raised in the tradition of selfless giving "for the sake of the kids," who now must create a family in a new, age segregated culture, viewers face a change in traditions that might otherwise go unnoticed. The hearty Shtetl elders, transplanted to Venice, California are forced to adapt their traditions yet again in their gentrifying neighborhood, celebrating the Sabbath at noon and New Years at two on the thirtieth. This film provides a great number of openings through which to crack the wall of "unchanging tradition," as well as who a family consists of, in a context familiar enough to most viewers to make them realize these ideas might apply to them. Viewers are also made participants/observers of anthropological fieldwork, as they observe Myerhoff in action and see and hear her interviewed regarding her research in the community. Ethnic identity is displayed through a variety of channels; e.g., language, dance, music, singing, religion, humor. But these Eastern European Jews have also become Americans, a great lead-in to discussions of the construction of identity. The filmmaker deploys strategies which engage the viewer emotionally through quick and dramatic shifts of mood, bringing an empathetic power to the message, for those inclined to discuss how film can work to get people to understand each other.

## QUESTIONS BEFORE SCREENING:

1. What is a diaspora? Examples?
2. What is ethnicity? What are components of ethnic identity? Is it biological?
3. How does tradition relate to the concept of ethnicity?
4. Is aging and death a common topic of interest in the U.S.? What about all those cop shows, horror and spy movies, and the news? Why is there such a focus on youth? Why are the elderly jettisoned?
5. What is anthropological fieldwork? What is the methodology? What do they learn from it?

QUESTIONS AFTER SCREENING:

1. Did this film reach you primarily on an emotional level or on an intellectual level? What techniques were used to do so?
2. What work does Barbara Myerhoff do, and how does she do it? What does she learn?
3. If they celebrate the Sabbath at noon instead of following the prescriptions of the Torah, are they following tradition?
4. What is a family? Many members of the community call themselves a family; are they? Why do they seem not to have biological families?
5. How would you identify them ethnically? Why not American? In what circumstances would you identify them as Americans?

Distributor: Direct Cinema Limited
*Note*: See distributor information at the end of the book.

\* \* \* \* \* \* \* \* \* \* \*

# PULL OURSELVES UP OR DIE OUT

John Marshall, filmmaker
Distributor: Documentary Educational Resources
Format: 16mm film, video, color, 20 minutes, 1985
Genre: classic ethnographic film
Key Words:     Southern Africa, !Kung, Ju/Æhoansi, Hunting and
               Gathering, Agriculture, Social Change, Conflict

SUMMARY:

*Pull Ourselves Up or Die Out* is a field report which provides visual and factual information on the situation of the !Kung San people at Tshum!Kwi, in Namibia, where N!ai, the Story of a !Kung Woman was filmed. The report includes footage shot at or near Tshum!Kwi between the years of 1980 and 1984 and was an outgrowth of research conducted by John Marshall and Claire Ritchie during those same years. Highlighted in the taped report are: problems and issues which affect the !Kung as the economy continues to shift from subsistence to cash-based; scenes and interviews surrounding the possible establishment of a game reserve in Eastern Bushmanland; development of cattle farming and husbandry by !Kung groups; confrontations with South African Administration officials regarding the rights to install a water pump and the rights of !Kung to use water.

REASONS FOR ITS USEFULNESS:

This film presents issues relating to the political economy of the Ju/Æhoansi, traditionally a hunting and gathering culture, as they continue to move towards an agricultural and animal farming economy. This film is part of one of the longest running documentation projects of a community. This film is useful when used in conjunction with other films like *The Hunters* and *Bitter Melons*.

QUESTIONS BEFORE SCREENING:

1. How would one define traditional?
2. What have been some of the obstacles to survival of traditional culture?

QUESTIONS AFTER SCREENING:

1. In relation to the theory of property of John Locke, what is the irony in the fact that the Ju/Æhoansi may lose rights to farm their land due to the designation of a game reserve?
2. What are some of the possible roles that an outsider like an anthropologist can place in indigenous politics? What are the ethical issues?

FILMS RELATED BY GEOGRAPHIC OR SUBJECT AREA:

The Hunters; The Meat Fight; A Joking Relationship; Bitter Melons; Num Tchai; An Argument about a Marriage; N!ai, the Story of a !Kung Woman, all by John Marshall

Reviews: Choice, April 1986, by P. Singer.
Associated Reading: The Cinema of John Marshall, edited by Jay Ruby, Philadelphia: Harwood Academic Publishers, 1993; The Harmless People, Elizabeth Marshall Thomas, New York: Alfred A. Knopf, 1959.

Distributor: Documentary Educational Resources
*Note*: See distributor information at the end of the book.

\* \* \* \* \* \* \* \* \* \* \*

## - 40 -

## THE FEAST

Tim Asch, filmmaker; Napoleon Chagnon, anthropologist
Distributor: Documentary Educational Resources
Format: 16mm, 1/2 VHS, color, 29 minutes, 1968
Genre: classic
Key Words:        Political Alliance, Ritual, Fictive Kinship, Reciprocity, Food Preparation

SUMMARY:

Describes how an alliance is formed between hostile Yanomamo Indian villages of southern Venezuela and northeastern Brazil through feasting, trading, dancing, and chanting. Recounts the feast and its preparation using natural sound with occasional superimposed translations. From the Yanomamo series.

REASONS FOR ITS USEFULNESS:

This film, accompanied by many others in the Yanomamo series, provides wide filmic coverage of this people. Though the documents are profoundly shaped by Chagnon's narrow paradigm of internal population genetics, a combination of critical awareness and anthropological insight can be built upon the recordings. This film can be used to examine concepts of ritual reciprocity and political alliance. While the initial "slide show" format gives detailed information about the participants, it also clearly lays out the interpretive paradigm used. The later observational portion, occasionally subtitled, gives the viewer more direct bits of "data" regarding the proceedings. This, along with the introductory map — a great boon — allows the viewer the potential to "read against the grain." The dangerous and fragile nature of treaties, the shifting winds of political partnership, and the difficulties inherent in giving and receiving are all highlighted. Missing, as with most of this series, is the relationship to anyone except other Yanomamo.

QUESTIONS BEFORE SCREENING:

1. What is a feast? Why do people feast? Who is typically invited?
2. Thanksgiving is a feast celebrating what alliance? Why is it still celebrated? What does it celebrate now, and who participates?
3. How have some of the U.S.'s political alliances changed over the past decade? Why?
4. What is reciprocity? Is it an important element of society in the U.S.? Are there class differences in its practice?
5. What is carrying capacity? How is it figured? What factors may lead to increases and decreases?

QUESTIONS AFTER SCREENING:

1. Why is the feast in the film important, according to the filmmakers? Do you have alternative suggestions?
2. What events are a part of the feast? How do these compare with a feast in the U.S.?
3. What forms of reciprocity do you see or hear about? Why are they important?
4. What are some of the political aspects of the feast? Are there changes to past political alignments?
5. What items of nonindigenous manufacture do you see in the film? How do you think these were obtained?

Distributor: Documentary Educational Resources
*Note*: See distributor information at the end of the book.

\* \* \* \* \* \* \* \* \* \*

# THE GODDESS AND THE COMPUTER

Stephen Lansing, anthropologist; Andre Singer, filmmaker
Distributor: Documentary Educational Resources
Format: video only (rental or purchase), color, 58 minutes, 1992
Genre: contemporary ethnographic film; film about ethnography
Key Words:   Bali, Irrigation, Development, Cyborg Anthropology,
              Fieldwork

SUMMARY:

For centuries, rice farmers on the island of Bali have taken great care not
to offend Dewi Danu, the water goddess who dwells in the crater lake near
the peak of Batur volcano. Toward the end of each rainy season, the
farmers send representatives to Ulun Danu Batur, the temple at the top of
the mountain, to offer ducks, pigs, coins, and coconuts in thanks for the
water that sustains their terraced fields. Outsiders have long considered
the rituals of Agama Tirtha, "the religion of holy water," an interesting
but impractical way to grow crops. Development companies have spent
millions trying to improve on the ancient system.

With the help of an ingenious computer program, anthropologist Stephen
Lansing and ecologist James Kremer have shown that the Balinese rice
growers have been practicing state-of-the-art resource management.
Besides placating the goddess, it turns out, the island's ancient rituals
serve to coordinate the irrigation and planting schedules of hundreds of
scattered villages. And as a new computer model makes clear, the result is
one of the most stable and efficient farming systems on the planet.

Andre Singer and Stephen Lansing have made an innovative film about
the water temples, the dams, and the development of the computer
program at the University of Southern California. In the film, we see the
government officials call on the priests and recognize the importance of
their role. We also see the power play as each group wants to control the
use of the computer.

## REASONS FOR ITS USEFULNESS:

In terms of its subject matter, water resource management, *The Goddess and the Computer* is a unique film. As one might expect, the film depicts and describes both the structure and workings of the "traditional" Balinese irrigation system. However, unlike structural-functionalists who might have treated this system as closed and static, Lansing and Singer focus upon the deleterious impact of exogenous forces — namely those unleashed by development agents in the form of the Green Revolution — upon the water temples and rice crops. In addressing the subject of change within culture, Lansing and Singer demonstrate that it is a negotiated process, and, as such, not inevitable. In fact, the film testifies to the important role that Lansing, himself, played in the conflict between water temple priests and farmers, on the one hand, and development and government officials, on the other, thereby making the point that practitioners of anthropology are often in the situations where they have a significant influence over the course of events. While the film does not directly address the ethics and responsibilities of applied anthropology, it certainly raises these as issues for the audience.

## QUESTIONS BEFORE SCREENING:

1. How would you define "traditional" culture?
2. How would you define "westernized" culture?
3. To what extent do these terms have validity?
4. What is the role of technology in society?
5. What is international development and who are its agents?

## QUESTIONS AFTER SCREENING:

1. How would you compare the relationship between religion and science in "traditional" Balinese society to that in "westernized" society?
2. Discuss some of the differences between the emic and etic understanding of "traditional" Balinese water resource management.
3. Give several examples of cultural diffusion as they appeared in this film.
4. What do you feel should be the anthropologist's role with respect to what he/she is studying? Documentarian? Activist? Mediator? etc.

86

5. Based upon this film, to what extent do you think international development is a successful/failed enterprise? Who benefits from development projects?

FILMS RELATED BY GEOGRAPHIC OR SUBJECT AREA:

Trance and Dance in Bali, by Margaret Mead and Gregory Bateson
Bathing Babies, by Margaret Mead and Gregory Bateson

Distributor: Documentary Educational Resources
          Contact: Cynthia Close
Note: See distributor information at the end of the book.

* * * * * * * * * * *

---

## - 42 -

## THE HUMAN PYRAMID

Jean Rouch, filmmaker
Distributor: Contact Documentary Educational Resources for latest information.
Format: 16mm film, video, color, 80 minutes, 1961
Genre: classic ethnographic film
Key Words: West Africa, Ivory Coast, Racism

SUMMARY:

This film elicits problems of interracial relations in a school in Abidjan, Ivory Coast. Students are first asked to pick roles for themselves that they will play in an acted film. A young black man and young white woman decide to be friends in the film. Others choose opposing and supporting sides around this half imagined, half real relationship. The film unfolds as differing configurations of those involved interact as they move through their real and fictional lives. The dramatic action revolves around portrayals of racism and reactions to them. A dramatic twist at the end unites the entire group around empathy for a fellow classmate. New interracial relationships emerge through the making of the film. A young black and a young white, who were racist toward each other before the project, became friends and change their attitudes about the other's race after the scripted portion of the drama ends.

REASONS FOR ITS USEFULNESS:

This film is path-breaking in its methodology. By asking nonactors to portray characters that may or may not be far from their own personalities, Jean Rouch succeeds in opening a dialogue that would be difficult to document in reality. His film is instrumental in the lives of the subjects of the film. Their participation forces them to think deeply about their own attitudes about race. As distant observers of the interactions, we — the viewers — are offered a lot to think about. How much of racism is a learned drama that we act out in our relationships? How easy is it to switch roles?

QUESTIONS BEFORE SCREENING:

1. What is race?
2. What is racism?

QUESTIONS AFTER SCREENING:

1. How might this film be different if it was made in America in 1961?
2. How is this film unique in its documentation and presentation of events?

FILMS RELATED BY GEOGRAPHIC OR SUBJECT AREA:

The Lion Hunters; Jaguar; Petit a Petit; Madame L'Eau, all by Jean Rouch

Associated Reading: The Cinematic Griot: the Ethnography of Jean Rouch, by Paul Stoller, Chicago: The University of Chicago Press, 1992.

Distributor: Documentary Educational Resources
Note: See distributor information at the end of the book.

\* \* \* \* \* \* \* \* \* \* \*

# 43

# THE HUNTERS

John Marshall, filmmaker
Distributor: Films Incorporated
Format: 16mm film, video, color, 80 minutes, 1957
Genre: classic ethnographic film
Key Words: Southern Africa !Kung, Ju/Æhoansi, Hunting and Gathering

## SUMMARY:

For tens of thousands of years the ancestors of the modern Ju/Æhoansi hunted and gathered bush foods in southern Africa. At the time of the making of this film, they were reduced to a few small bands in the Kalahari desert and indentured servants on farms of other ethnic groups including European colonists. This film is about hunting and gathering in one of the bands in Nyae Nyae. It follows the story of an ordinary hunt over several days. It is a creative form of documentary where actuality footage is used to tell a truthful, yet somewhat fictionalized, narrative.

Four men leave their families and band for five days to gather bush foods and hunt large game. They track a pod of giraffes and successfully puncture a large female with a small poison arrow. For the next three days they track the giraffe over miles of desert terrain, living off of bush foods and a large porcupine they spear. The tracks and spoor of the dying giraffe are interpreted by the expert hunters and lead them successfully to their quarry. The four men spear the several ton giraffe and bring it down.

## REASONS FOR ITS USEFULNESS:

From the emergence of modern Homo Sapiens some 300,000 years ago until around 10,000 years ago, all cultures' primary mode of subsistence was hunting and gathering. In the last few thousand years, through cultural diffusion and independent invention, most cultures have institutionalized other modes like pastoralism, horticulture, agriculture, and industry. However, the sometimes difficult but often quite luxurious life style of hunting and gathering was still practiced by several groups until very recently. This film is useful in that it deals with this ancient traditional form of food supplementation from the perspective of ethnographic observation. John Marshall was intimate with these men and their families for years prior to the making of this film, and the film is an honest portrayal of hunting events. The film can be shown successfully with other films in the series including *The Meat Fight* and *!Kung Bushmen Hunting Equipment*.

QUESTIONS BEFORE SCREENING:

1. What is the nature of the knowledge necessary for survival in a hunting and gathering community and how is it attained?
2. What is the relationship between a community's mode of subsistence and its social organization, language, religion, and arts?

QUESTIONS AFTER SCREENING:

1. What are some of the possible principles of distribution of the meat of a kill like the one depicted in the film?
2. At the time of the photographing of this film, how would the limiting of the Ju/Æhoansi's hunting territory by outside forces effect their survival?

FILMS RELATED BY GEOGRAPHIC OR SUBJECT AREA:

The Meat Fight; An Argument about a Marriage; A Joking Relationship; Bitter Melons; N/um Tchai; N!ai, The Story of a !Kung Woman; Pull Ourselves Up or Die Out, all by John Marshall

Awards: American Film Festival, Blue Ribbon
Reviews: American Anthropologist, March 1980, by Bill Nichols
Associated Reading: The Cinema of John Marshall, edited by Jay Ruby, Philadelphia: Harwood Academic Publishers, 1993; The Harmless People, Elizabeth Marshall Thomas, New York: Alfred A. Knopf, 1959.

Distributor: Films Incorporated
*Note*: See distributor information at the end of the book.

* * * * * * * * * *

# 44

# THE JAPANESE VERSION

Louis Alvarez and Andrew Kolker, filmmakers
Distributor: Center for New American Media
Format: video, color, 56 minutes, 1991
Genre: classic ethnographic film
Key Words:       Japan, Assimilation, United States, Contemporary
                 Industrial/Service Society

SUMMARY:

Two American social scientists are interested in how the West gets
assimilated in Japan. They interview Japanese engaged in all types of
activities and observe many different aspects of Japanese society relating
to the issue of cultural borrowing from the United States. They also
interview Western experts on Japan. Material includes Japanese baseball,
love hotels with Western theme rooms, Western wedding ceremonies, a
country and Western bar with Japanese in cowboy clothing singing
country music, Western products with a Japanese twist, a cherry blossom
viewing where participants discuss Japanese/American competition, and a
game show that moves into final rounds in the U.S.

REASONS FOR ITS USEFULNESS:

This video offers a good introduction to both contemporary Japanese
society and the issues of cultural assimilation. Though the film does not
deal with traditional Japanese society by dealing with current maintenance
of cultural practices like Kabuki or Tea Ceremony, it does deal with
tradition in how it interacts with cultural borrowings to produce new
forms. The Japanese have had a long tradition of modifying things that
they have learned from other cultures to suit their own particular
sensibilities and needs. It is interesting for Westerners to reflect on what
they take for granted when they see it in the Japanese version. This film
helps Americans to see our own culture in a new light.

QUESTIONS BEFORE SCREENING:

1. What is assimilation?
2. Where does Japan fit in the First World/Third World dichotomy, and how does it challenge the validity of this categorization?

QUESTIONS AFTER SCREENING:

1. What are some of the patterns of transformation of Western cultural forms in their Japanese versions?
2. What does one learn about Western society from this film?

FILMS RELATED BY GEOGRAPHIC OR SUBJECT AREA:

Neighborhood Tokyo, by Theodore Bestor

Associated Reading: Neighborhood Tokyo, by Theodore Bestor, Stanford, CA: Stanford University Press, 1989.

Distributor: Center for New American Media
Note: See distributor information at the end of the book.

* * * * * * * * * *

## - 45 -

## THE LION HUNTERS

Jean Rouch, filmmaker
Distributor: Documentary Educational Resources
Format: 16mm film, video, color, 88 minutes, 1964
Genre: classic ethnographic film
Key Words:     West Africa, Niger, Mali, Fulani, Songhay, Hunting,
                Magic, Guilds, Storytelling

## SUMMARY:

Footage for this film was collected over a seven year period during the 1950s and 1960s, among the Fulani herdsmen and Songhay villagers in the Savannah of northern Niger and Mali. The Songhay call this region "the bush which is farther than far the land of nowhere." The Songhay were the dominant people of a formerly powerful kingdom, destroyed in the sixteenth century, that stretched along the Niger River from the edge of the Sahara to the rain forests in the south. The Songhay today are millet farmers and are still considered to own the land on which Fulani herdsman have rights of pastorage. Songhay also own the land's game, including lions.

Lion-hunting is reserved by tradition to the Gao, a group of Songhay-speaking professional hunters, masters of the techniques and rituals of poison-making. The Gao also possess great knowledge of the bush and are thought to have a special relationship with the spirits that inhabit its trees and waters. When lions raid Fulani cattle, the Fulani must request that Songhay chiefs send Gao hunters to their aid. The Songhay chiefs are paid by the Fulani in cattle. The Gao receive the lion's skin, skull, and other parts, including the heart which can command up to $1,000 in coastal cities where it is used in medicine and ritual.

Lions generally kill only sick or injured cattle, but on occasion they will attack a healthy herd. The Gao are usually able to determine which lion is responsible, for they know the characteristics and habits of individual animals. In the film, for example, the hunters attempt to find "The American," so called because of its strength and cleverness. Although lion hunting is a test of manly courage, the Gao sing the praises, not only of the hunters but also the hunted, following a kill. Once trapped and shot with poison arrows, the lion is commanded to die quickly and to forgive the hunters. Its body is struck three times to liberate the animal's soul, so that it will not drive the hunters mad.

## REASONS FOR ITS USEFULNESS:

The film follows not only several hunts, including one in which an inexperienced Fulani is seriously wounded by a cornered lion, but also the technology of the hunt. Bows are cut from forest trees, metal arrow points are forged, and poison is made from the seeds of the "poison tree." This tree, also called the "mother of magic," is found in the bush some 300 miles south of the Gao homeland. Every four years the Gao hunters travel to this area, where they prepare the poison within a "magic circle." The seeds are boiled in water while spells are recited. Upon return to Gao country, traps are set with perfume bottles buried under piles of pebbles, for lions, the Gao explain, are like girls, adoring perfume.

The relationships between the Gao, other Songhay-speakers, and the Fulani herdsmen are intriguing. Perhaps, as Rouch suggests, the Gao serve as mediators between an ancient hunting way of life, with its spirits of the bush, and the life and gods of pastoralism and settled agriculture. One may also speculate on the economic, social, and political relationships that are sustained or even created through the lion hunt.

QUESTIONS BEFORE SCREENING:

1.  Why is it important to understand the histories of various cultures' relationships?
2.  What is meant by the "division of labor in society?"

QUESTIONS AFTER SCREENING:

1.  What is the nature of the specialized knowledge and schooling of the Gao?
2.  Are the Gao cultural elites among the Songhay? Among the Fulani?

FILMS RELATED BY GEOGRAPHIC OR SUBJECT AREA:

Jaguar; La Pyramide Humaine; Petit a Petit; Madame L'Eau, all by Jean Rouch

Awards: Golden Lion at the XXVI Venice Film Festival, 1965.
Associated Reading: The Cinematic Griot: the Ethnography of Jean Rouch, by Paul Stoller, Chicago: The University of Chicago Press, 1992.

Distributor: Documentary Educational Resources
*Note*: See distributor information at the end of the book.
\* \* \* \* \* \* \* \* \* \* \*

# 46

# THE MEAT FIGHT

John Marshall, filmmaker
Distributor: Documentary Educational Resources
Format: 16mm film, video, color, 14 minutes, 1974
Genre: classic ethnographic film
Key Words:    Southern Africa, !Kung, Ju/Æhoansi, Hunting and
              Gathering, Conflict, Distribution

## SUMMARY:

Though short, this film is packed with cultural detail. It is often through
analysis of the abnormal situations like the one depicted in the film that
we get a clear idea of what is normal for a culture. The rules of meat
distribution are usually quite automatic in their execution, but this caseùa
man finds an animal wounded by a man from another band leads to
conflict and the resolution of that conflict in a moot presided over by
senior members of the band. In the end they decide to share the meat with
the band of the man who initially wounded the animal. The film illustrates
how leadership is enacted in a community with loose forms of political
organization and how violence is avoided through negotiation and decision
making.

## REASONS FOR ITS USEFULNESS:

Hunting and gathering communities are rarely every person for
themselves. In fact, one finds just the opposite in every case of hunting
and gathering documented by ethnographers. One finds a high degree of
interdependence. Food and other properties are shared in a social network.
The sharing process is not static, however, but is negotiated over time
often involving conflict. Though having no formal political system,
kinship, age, and gender differences are important in Ju/Æhoansi society
as well as are merit and charisma. In this film, a difficult case of
ownership rights is adjudicated by important members of a community,
enhancing group solidarity, ties to other bands, and the symbolic capital of
the participants in the conflict. Crisis is averted through dialogue. Though

no written laws come into play, one does get the sense that this community has a complex set of laws and that there are analogous processes to the Western justice system at work in this hunting and gathering society.

QUESTIONS BEFORE SCREENING:

1. What are the principles or logic of meat distribution in Ju/Æhoansi society?
2. How do Ju/Æhoansi mechanism of conflict resolution differ from our own, and how are they similar?
3. What do we learn about social organization from the film?

QUESTIONS AFTER SCREENING:

1. What does the film tell us about how a logical system like meat distribution gets created and maintained?
2. How does this film challenge or support the myth that the life of a hunter and gatherer is simple?

FILMS RELATED BY GEOGRAPHIC OR SUBJECT AREA:

The Hunters; An Argument about a Marriage; A Joking Relationship; Bitter Melons; N/um Tchai; N!ai, The Story of a !Kung Woman; Pull Ourselves Up or Die Out, all by John Marshall

Reviews: American Anthropologist, 76:3, September, pg. 689-691, by Patricia Draper.
Associated Reading: The Cinema of John Marshall, edited by Jay Ruby, Philadelphia: Harwood Academic Publishers, 1993; The Harmless People, Elizabeth Marshall Thomas, New York: Alfred A. Knopf, 1959.

Distributor: Documentary Educational Resources
*Note*: See distributor information at the end of the book.

* * * * * * * * * * *

# 47

# THE PEYOTE ROAD

Fidel Moreno, director; Kifaru Productions
Distributor: Documentary Educational Resources
Format: video only (rent or purchase), color, 59 minutes, 1993
Genre: contemporary
Key Words:     Native Americans, Religion, Rites, Constitutional
                     Jurisprudence, Ethnocentrism, Native American Paintings

SUMMARY:

*The Peyote Road* addresses the United Stated Supreme Court "Smith"
decision, which denied protection of First Amendment religious liberty to
the sacramental use of Peyote for Indigenous people, one of the oldest
tribal religions in the Western Hemisphere. Examining the European
tradition of religious intolerance and documenting the centuries old
sacramental use of the cactus Peyote, *The Peyote Road* explains how the
"Smith" decision put religious freedom in jeopardy for all Americans.
This program contributed to the successful efforts of the American Indian
Religious Freedom Coalition, resulting in the passage of the historic 1994
amendment to The American Indian Religious Freedom Act.

REASONS FOR ITS USEFULNESS:

On one level, this film is primarily concerned with religious freedom;
however, on another level, *The Peyote Road* addresses the more
generalized issue of cultural difference and the conflicts that arise from it.
Consequently, meaning can be extracted from this film that would be
applicable to a wide range of subjects, of which religion is but one. The
film intimates that, just as restrictions imposed on the Native American
Church could impact negatively upon other religions practiced in the
United States, the refusal to acknowledge and legitimate the existence of
culturally rooted differences could have undesirable consequences for
minority (and indirectly majority) groups, not merely in the realm of
religion but, in all areas of life, be they public or private. An important
part of the argument for the legalized use of peyote within the Native

American Church is based upon the concept of cultural relativism and the corollary belief that each society has a cultural logic of its own that organizes and relates all of its constitutive parts. As an illustration of this, the film contrasts the different approaches taken by the United States government and the Native American Church toward the ingestion of peyote, and, in the process, demonstrates that, although both groups may be speaking about the same object, they are doing so in fundamentally different ways with fundamentally different underlying presumptions. Whereas many representatives of the U.S. government categorize peyote as a "drug," members of the Native American Church perceive it as a "medicine." In short, they do not speak the same language. While the film follows the story of the struggle over peyote legalization to its, as of yet, successful conclusion, it does not provide an easy resolution to the issue. Rather, it encourages the audience to delve into the very meaning and usage of much-employed, yet little considered, words such as "drug," "medicine," "religion," and "ritual," and it challenges the audience to reflect upon the hegemonic, yet unsatisfactory, character of scientific rationalism as it has taken shape in the United States.

QUESTIONS BEFORE SCREENING:

1. What is the meaning of indigenous, and to which ethnic groups would this term apply? In your opinion, in which historical era do you think this word entered the English language?
2. What is religious syncretism?
3. What is a sacrament? Give several examples.
4. Discuss both the connotative and denotative meanings of "history" and "prehistory."
5. In your opinion, define what you think the word "drug" should refer to, and cite your reasons.

QUESTIONS AFTER SCREENING:

1. Discuss the consequences that the Supreme Court's 1990 Smith ruling had for members of the Native American Church, as well as for members of other religions practiced here in the United States.
2. In emic terms, describe the reasons for using peyote during religious ceremonies.

3. What social functions/purposes can be served by religion? What role might religion play in a society that is undergoing tremendous trauma and change?
4. What role have missionaries played in the lives of Native Americans, and how have they influenced Native Americans' religious practices?
5. Based on the film, select an instance of cultural diffusion and discuss it.

## FILMS RELATED BY GEOGRAPHIC OR SUBJECT AREA:

Lighting the Seventh Fire, by Sandra Osawa

Awards: Birmingham International Educational Film EST, "Best 9-Adult," 1994
National Educational Film Fest, "Silver Apple" Award, 1994
C.I.N.E., "Golden Eagle" Award, 1994
Chicago International Film Festival, "Silver Plaque" Award, 1993
Great Plains Film Festival, "Best Documentary" Award, 1993
New York Festivals, "Silver Medal" Award, 1993
Parnu Anthropology Festival, "Best Educational Film," 1992

Distributor: Documentary Educational Resources
            Contact: Cynthia Close
Distributor: Kifaru Productions
Note: See distributor information at the end of the book.

\* \* \* \* \* \* \* \* \* \*

# TROBRIAND CRICKET: AN INGENIOUS RESPONSE TO COLONIALISM

Gary Kildea, director; Jerry Leach, producer
Distributor: University of California Extension Media Center (UCEMC)
Format: 16mm film, video (rent or purchase), color, 53 minutes, 1976
Genre: contemporary
Key Words:    Acculturation, Diffusion, Islands of the Pacific, Papua
New Guinea, Politics, Ritual

SUMMARY:

An ethnographic documentary about cultural creativity among the Trobriand Islanders of Papua New Guinea. Shows how the Trobrianders have taken the very controlled game of British cricket, first introduced by missionaries, and changed it into an outlet for mock warfare and intervillage competition; political reputation building among leaders; erotic dancing and chanting; and riotous fun. The game is a gigantic nonverbal message about people's attitudes and experiences under colonialism.

REASONS FOR ITS USEFULNESS:

*Trobriand Cricket* is very useful as a pedagogical tool for a number of reasons. First, in taking culture change as its primary topic, it addresses a subject that is rarely foregrounded by documentary and ethnographic films, but which is essential to any holistic study of cultural phenomena. Second, *Trobriand Cricket* touches upon another profoundly universal feature of culture — ritualized behavior — in its depiction and narration of each stage of the cricket match as played by Trobrianders. Third, while not addressing the specific shape and content of Trobriand politics, the film plainly points out the political nature of its subject by inquiring into the nature of relations between the participants, be they active (players and organizers) or passive (audience). Finally, the film's balanced blend of cultural specificity and cultural universality satisfies the audience's thirst for descriptions and facts, while simultaneously imparting to it ideas and concepts that will be highly useful in other contexts.

## QUESTIONS BEFORE SCREENING:

1. What can games or sports tell an anthropologist about the society in which they are played?
2. To what political/economic practice does the word "colonialism" refer? Discuss some of its consequences for both the colonial power and the colonial subject.
3. What do anthropologists mean by the phrase "cultural diffusion?"
4. Name and discuss several forms that cultural resistance has and can take.
5. What is the distinction between acculturation and assimilation?

## QUESTIONS AFTER SCREENING:

1. Describe the relationship between Trobriand warfare (before it was banned by the Papuan government) and Trobriand cricket.
2. How did missionaries help spread colonial influence and power in the Trobriand islands?
3. What might be some of the positive social benefits of ceremonial food exchange?
4. What type of person/village is most likely to sponsor cricket games and why?
5. If neither side is publicly acknowledged to be the winner, then why do they take the game so seriously?

## FILMS RELATED BY GEOGRAPHIC OR SUBJECT AREA:

Trobriand Islanders of Papua New Guinea, by Annette Weiner; Disappearing World Series, Films Incorporated, 1990

Awards: Blue Ribbon Winner, American Film Festival

Distributor: University of California Extension Media Center (UCEMC)
            Contact: Kate Spohr
*Note*: See distributor information at the end of the book.

\* \* \* \* \* \* \* \* \* \*

# VEILED REVOLUTION

Marilyn Gaunt, director; Elizabeth Fernea, producer
Distributor: First Run Features/Icarus Films
Format: 16mm, 1/2 VHS, color, 27 minutes, 1982
Genre: contemporary
Key Words: Clothing, Veil, Sharia, Visual Communication

SUMMARY:

*Veiled Revolution* attempts to discern the reasons behind the movement in Egypt by young, educated women to resume wearing traditional Islamic garb, sometimes with full face veil and gloves, despite a long history of feminine activism in Egypt. Asks: Is it an echo of the Iranian revolution? Is it a rejection of Western values? Considers the personal, socioreligious, and political implications of the movement. From the Women in the Middle East series.

REASONS FOR ITS USEFULNESS:

While viewers may have encountered women in their community who practice various forms of modesty, including wearing veils, it is doubtful they understand the wide range of meanings it may have. This film explores the range of dress in Egyptian society interjecting a variety of potential reasons for dressing in a particular way ranging from personal to political, gendered to religious. The film stimulates viewers to consider how the apparently simple act of clothing oneself can be viewed as an elaborate form of communication, demanding attention to present context as well as historical continuity, in order to properly decode the message. In addition, the women in the film express a variety of reactions to various possibilities now offered them in style of dress as well as very different reactions to what dressing in a particular fashion may mean. Caught between contradictory currents of appearing modern and feminist, yet being resistant to Western fashions and expensive imports, feeling protected from the male "gaze" and wearing homemade clothes tied to "restrictive," gendered religious law, these women each find personal solutions to the problem of what to wear. It opens viewers to a very different perspective on the importance of clothing as a subsistence need, opening their senses to the rich stew of cultural symbols simmering about them.

## QUESTIONS BEFORE SCREENING:

1. What needs do clothes serve?
2. What messages can you read about people from what they wear?
3. How do people select what to wear? What are some social and cultural (legal, religious, gender, age, class, etc.) factors involved in getting dressed?
4. What regions of the body is it appropriate to cover or leave uncovered? What are ways of covering them? How does this change cross-culturally?
5. What is a veil? Why do women in certain cultures wear them?

## QUESTIONS AFTER SCREENING:

1. What different reasons were given in the film for wearing veils? What reasons were given for not wearing veils?
2. Why did women want to adopt western styles of dress? What are some of the problems with dressing like this now?
3. How do differences between the class, social status, religion, age of the women effect their ideas about clothing styles?
4. Why do you think the film only touches on how women dress?
5. Why is this film important to us in the West? How do the issues in the film relate to issues over appearance in the U.S.?

Distributor: First Run Features/Icarus Films
*Note*: See distributor information at the end of the book.

* * * * * * * * * *

# 50

# WHOSE PAINTINGS?

Jayasinhji Jhala and Lindsey Powell, producer/directors
Distributor: Documentary Educational Resources
Format: 1/2 VHS, color, 45 minutes, 1995
Genre: contemporary
Key Words:    Cultural Aesthetics, Collecting, Ownership, Patrimony,
               Art, Material Culture

SUMMARY:

*Whose Paintings?* takes an ethnographic approach to recording an encounter between Alwin Belak, a Russian Jewish-American collector of sixteenth to nineteenth century miniature paintings from Rajput India, and Jayasinhji Jhala, a Rajput visual anthropologist from India, teaching at Temple University in Philadelphia. Part confrontation and part collaboration, the event of viewing these paintings in a Philadelphia apartment demonstrates the different points of view used by the two protagonists to engage with these cultural treasures. The emphasis of the art collector and the native ethnographer compliment and speak past each other. This dynamic film — while providing particular information and insight about the subjects of art collecting, Rajput aesthetics, history, social custom, and culture — suggests by the silent refrain generated by the discourse, inquiry into questions of cultural patrimony.

REASONS FOR ITS USEFULNESS:

It has become commonplace to hear of artifacts and art pieces selling for millions of dollars. In fact it seems everything is for sale and anything may be collectable. This film calls a brief halt to the bidding and investigates the phenomena. Viewers are given two contrasting perspectives on a collection of Rajput paintings. Both men seem to have an intimate connection with the art objects, yet there is a palpable tension over the "ownership." Clearly money determines ownership in the current art market, and avid collectors may possess a detailed understanding of particular objects or collections of objects. This film conveys to the viewers a palpable sense of a more elusive sort of ownership; of enculturation; of shared participation in values, beliefs, and customs expressed aesthetically; of a lived historical connection to the events embodied in an image. The filmic structure itself is a redundant expression of these aesthetic values, subtly reinforcing the innate, ingrained nature of culture as a set of preferences. From the ongoing discussion emerges a copious body of information about Indian cultural practices from religious beliefs to historical figures.

QUESTIONS BEFORE SCREENING:

1. What is art? When is something art? What is artisanal or artful?
2. What does art express? Do all cultures produce art? What is the relationship between culture and art? What are aesthetics?
3. Is there a difference between being bilingual and bicultural? What is it. How would it affect your interactions in a different culture.
4. Do you collect any sorts of objects? Why? What do you feel they express? Do you possess them, or do they somehow possess you?
5. What are different kinds of relationships people have with things? What are some class differences in this relationship?

QUESTIONS AFTER SCREENING:

1. How are the paintings in the film different from paintings in our culture?
2. How is the value of these paintings measured? How do they gain or loose value?
3. Characterize Alwin Belak's relationship to his painting collection? How does it differ from Jhala's relationship to them?
4. Who do you think should own these paintings? Why?
5. How are the two men seen in the film? Does it reflect the paintings in any way? Why do you think the authors made it like this?

Distributor: Documentary Educational Resources
Note: See distributor information at the end of the book.

* * * * * * * * * *

# 51

# WITHOUT RESERVATIONS:
# NOTES ON RACISM IN MONTANA

Produced by No Excuses Productions
Distributor: Native Voices Public Television
Format: 1/2 VHS, color, 28 minutes, 1995
Genre: indigenous video
Key Words: Indian, White, Racism, Stereotype, History

SUMMARY:

*Without Reservations: Notes on Racism in Montana* is a documentary that addresses questions of racism between whites and Indians in a new and bold manner. Weaving together brief interviews and shots of "popular" uses of the stereotypical Indian, the video explores race through the lives of a white/Indian couple, a reservation elementary school teacher who is Indian, and an Indian police officer. Their statements demonstrate the heterogeneity of Indians, attest to the perseverance of racism against Indians, and express their hopes to live in a world free of racism.

This tape is a perfect starter to introduce viewers to "real" Indians as well as persistent problems Indians continue to have living amidst white society. The film moves viewers quickly through a parade of paraphernalia deploying the stereotypic Indian as a representative for everything from a good night's sleep to a tough baseball team. This is intercut with statements by whites who see no racism around them. The life stories of Indians which follow quickly alert the viewer to a continuing legacy of persecution and discrimination, something many may think is part of the past. Connecting the present to history powerfully illuminates the present plight of many Native Americans and serves as ground for a reinterpretation of the romanticized and maligned "savage." The three longer stories situate racism in personal lives presenting different perspectives on both the problems and their solutions, as the protagonists of each story positively resolve their immediate problems. Yet, it is also clear the underlying problem of discrimination continues. The viewer's involvement on a very personal level with institutional racism, a problem which may seem abstract and overwhelming in conceptual terms, provides a sturdy bridge to grasp the "other's" point of view.

## QUESTIONS BEFORE SCREENING:

1. What are some common images that come to mind when thinking about Indians?
2. Do you think some of these images are stereotypes? Do you think some are racist?
3. How are Indians different from whites? Are these racial differences?
4. What is race? What is racism? What is institutional racism?
5. Do you think that racial discrimination against Indian peoples exists in the U.S. today? What forms does it take?

## QUESTIONS AFTER SCREENING:

1. What stereotypes of Indians does the film present? What kind of person do these construct?
2. How are the "real" Indians in the film different from the stereotypes?
3. What kinds of discrimination do the Indian people in the film confront? Do you think it's real or imagined?
4. How does the present condition of these Indian people relate to their historical past?
5. Why do you think the white people in the film do not perceive things in the same ways that the Indians do?

Distributor: Native Voices Public Television
*Note*: See distributor information at the end of the book.

* * * * * * * * * *

# DISTRIBUTOR INFORMATION

**C.R.M. Films**
2233 Faraday Avenue, Suite F
Carlsbad, CA 92008
    Phone: 619-431-9800

**California Newsreel**
149 Ninth Street
San Francisco, CA 94103
    Phone: 415-621-6196

**Center for New American Media**

**Compagnie France Film**
Place du Cercle
505 est, rue Sherbrooke, Bureau 2401
Montreal, Quebeck H2L 4N3
CANADA
    Phone: 514-844-0680

**Direct Cinema Limited**
Post Office Box 69799
Los Angeles, CA 90069
    Phone: 310-636-8200
    Fax: 310-636-8228

**Documentary Educational Resources**
101 Morse Street
Watertown, MA 02172
    Phone: 617-926-0492 or 800-569-6621
    Fax: 617-929-9519 (can send a purchase order by Fax)
    E-mail: docued@der.org
    URL: http://der.org/docued/

**Films for the Humanities, Inc.**
Post Office Box 2053
Princeton, NJ 08543
    Phone: 800-257-5126

**Films Incorporated**
5547 North Ravenswood
Chicago, IL 60640
    Phone: 800-323-4222
    http:\\publicmedia.com\fientertainment
    Contact:    June Widdowson, ext. 324

**First Run Features/Icarus Films**
153 Waverly Place
New York, NY 10014
    Phone: 212-727-1711
    Fax: 212-989-7649

**Independent Television Service**

**Kifaru Productions**
1550 California Street, Suite #275
San Francisco, CA 94109
    Phone: 800-400-VIDEO

**Mystic Fire Video**
P.O. Box 422
New York, NY 10012
    Phone: 212-941-0999
    Fax: 800-621-1699
    E-mail: mysticfire@echonyc.com
    URL: http://www.mysticfire.com

**New Day Films**
121 West 27th Street, $902
New York, NY 10001
    Phone: 212-645-8210

**University of California Media Extension Center**
University of California
2176 Shattuck Avenue
Berkeley, CA 94720
    Phone: 510-642-4124

**Upstream Productions**
420 First Avenue West
Seattle, WA 98119